OUT & ABOUT

• WALKING GUIDES TO BRITAIN •

No 5

South West England

MARSHALL CAVENDISH

First published in Great Britain in 1995 by
Marshall Cavendish Books, London
(a division of Marshall Cavendish Partworks Ltd)

Copyright © 1995 Marshall Cavendish

ISBN 03190 057 71

British Library Cataloguing in Publication Data:
A catalogue record for this book is available from the British Library

Printed and bound in Dubai, U.A.E.

Some of this material has previously appeared in the Marshall Cavendish partwork OUT & ABOUT

While every effort has been made to check the accuracy of these walks, neither Marshall Cavendish nor Ordnance Survey can be held
responsible for any errors or omissions, nor for any consequences arising from the use of information contained in this book.
Marshall Cavendish welcomes readers' letters pointing out changes that have taken place in land ownership, access, etc,
or inaccuracies in the walks' routes or descriptions.

CONTENTS

Introduction to
OUT & ABOUT
• WALKING GUIDES TO BRITAIN •

Walking has become one of the most popular pastimes in Britain. To enjoy walking, you don't need any special skills, you don't have to follow rules or join expensive clubs, and you don't need any special equipment – though a pair of walking boots is a good idea! It is an easy way of relaxing and getting some exercise, and of enjoying nature and the changing seasons.

The OUT & ABOUT WALKING GUIDES TO BRITAIN will give you ideas for walks in your own neighbourhood and in other areas of Britain. All the walks are devised around a theme and range in length from about 2 to 9 miles (3.25 to 14.5 km) and in difficulty from very easy to mildly strenuous. Since each walk is circular, you will always be able to get back to your starting point.

Devised by experts and tested for accuracy, all the walks are accompanied by clear, practical instructions and an enlarged section of the relevant Ordnance Survey map. The flavour of the walk and highlights to look out for are described in the introductory text.

LOCAL COLOUR

Background features give you extra insight into items of local interest. The OUT & ABOUT WALKING GUIDES TO BRITAIN relate legends, point out unusual architectural details, provide a potted history of the lives of famous writers and artists connected with a particular place, explain traditional crafts still practised by local artisans, and uncover the secrets behind an ever-changing landscape.

DISCOVER NATURE

One of the greatest pleasures in going for a walk is the sense of being close to nature. On the walks suggested in the OUT & ABOUT WALKING GUIDES TO BRITAIN, you can feel the wind, smell the pine trees, hear the birds and see the beauty of the countryside. You will become more aware of the seasons – the life cycles of butterflies, the mating calls of birds, the protective behaviour of all creatures with their young. You will see the beginning of new life in the forests and fields, the bluebell carpets in spring woodlands, the dazzling beauty of rhododendron bushes in early summer, the swaying cornfields of summer and the golden colours of leaves in autumn. The OUT & ABOUT WALKING GUIDES TO BRITAIN tell you what to look out for and where to find it.

NATURE WALK

Occasional nature walk panels. will highlight an interesting feature that you will see on your walk. You will learn about natural and manmade details in the landscape, how to tell which animal or bird has nibbled the cones in a pine forest, what nurse trees are and what a triangulation point is.

FACT FILE

The fact file will give you at-a-glance information about each walk to help you make your selection.

⚹ **general location**

OS **map reference for Ordnance Survey**
   map with grid reference for starting point

miles 0 1 2 3 4 5 6 7 8 9 **length of the walk in**
kms 0 1 2 3 4 5 6 7 8 9 10 11 12 13 14 15 **miles and kilometres**

◔ **time needed if walking at an average speed**

▬ **character of the walk: easy/easy with**
◼ **strenuous parts/mildly strenuous; hills to**
▲ **be climbed and muddy or dangerous**
   areas are pointed out

P **parking facilities near the start of the walk**

T **public transport information**

🍺 **facilities for refreshment, including pubs**
🍴 **serving lunchtime meals, restaurants, tea**
   rooms and picnic areas

WC **location of toilets**

⌐⊓ **historic sites**

ORDNANCE SURVEY MAPS

All the walks in the OUT & ABOUT WALKING GUIDES TO BRITAIN are illustrated on large-scale, full-colour maps supplied by the Ordnance Survey. Ordnance Survey are justifiably proud of their worldwide reputation for excellence and accuracy. For extra clarity, the maps have been enlarged to a scale of 1:21,120 (3 inches to 1 mile).

The route for each walk is marked clearly on the map with a broken red line, and the numbers along the

ABOVE: *Colourful narrowboats are always an attractive feature on inland waterways.*

route refer you to the numbered stages in the written directions. In addition, points of interest are marked on the maps with letters. Each one is mentioned in the walk directions and is described in detail in the introductory text.

COUNTRYWISE

The countryside is one of our greatest resources. If we treat it with respect, we can preserve it for the future.

Throughout the countryside there is a network of paths and byways. Some are former trading routes, others are simply the paths villagers took to visit one another in the days before public transport. Most are designated 'rights of way': foot-paths, open only to people on foot, and bridleways, open to people on foot, horseback or bicycle. These paths can be identified on Ordnance Survey maps and verified, in cases of dispute, by the definitive map for the area, held by the relevant local authority.

THE LAW OF TRESPASS

If you find a public right of way barred to you, you may remove the obstruction or take a short detour around it. However, in England and Wales, if you stray from the footpath you are trespassing and could be sued in a civil court for damages. In Scotland, rights of way are not recorded on definitive maps, nor is there a law of trespass. Although you may cross mountain and moorland paths, landowners are permitted to impose restrictions on access, such as during the grouse-shooting season, which should be obeyed.

If you are following a public right of way and find, for example, that your path is blocked by a field of crops, you are entitled to walk the line of the footpath through the crops, in single file. Farmers are required, by law, to restore public rights of way within 14 days of ploughing. However, if you feel uncomfortable about doing this and can find a way round, then do so. But report the matter to the local authority who will take the necessary action to clear the correct route.

RIGHT: *The stunning patchwork of fields surrounding the picturesque village of Widecombe in the heart of Dartmoor makes a beautiful setting for the famous annual fair.*
BELOW: *Brown hares boxing in spring are a fascinating sight.*

It is illegal for farmers to place a bull on its own in a field crossed by a right of way (unless the bull is not a recognized dairy breed). If you come across a bull alone in a field, find another way round.

COMMONS AND PARKS

There are certain areas in England and Wales where you may be able to wander without keeping to paths, such as most commons and beaches. There are also country parks, set up by local authorities for public recreation – parkland, woodland, heath or farmland.

The National Trust is the largest private landowner in England and Wales. Its purpose is to preserve areas of natural beauty and sites of historic interest by acquisition, holding them in trust for public access and enjoyment. Information on access may be obtained from National Trust headquarters at

THE COUNTRY CODE

- **Enjoy the countryside, and respect its life and work**
- **Always guard against risk of fire**
- **Fasten all gates**
- **Keep your dogs under close control**
- **Keep to public footpaths across farmland**
- **Use gates and stiles to cross fences, hedges and walls**
- **Leave livestock, crops and machinery alone**
- **Take your litter home**
- **Help to keep all water clean**
- **Protect wildlife, plants and trees**
- **Take special care on country roads**
- **Make no unnecessary noise**

36 QueenAnne's Gate, London SW1H 9AS
Tel: 071-222 9251.

ABOVE RIGHT *Carelessness with cigarettes, matches or camp fires can be devastating in a forest.*

Most regions of great scenic beauty in England and Wales are designated National Parks or Areas of Outstanding Natural Beauty (AONB). In Scotland, they are known as National Scenic Areas (NSAs) or AONBs.

Most of this land is privately owned and there is no right of public access. In some cases, local authorities may have negotiated agreements with landowners to allow walkers access on mountains and moors.

CONSERVATION

National park, AONB or NSA status is intended to provide some measure of protection for the land-scape, guarding against unsuitable development while encouraging enjoyment of its natural beauty.

Nature reserves are areas set aside for conservation. Most are privately owned, some by large organizations such as the Royal Society for the Protection of Birds. Although some offer public access, most require permission to enter.

THE RAMBLERS ASSOCIATION

The aims of the Ramblers Association are to further greater understanding and care of the countryside, to protect and enhance public rights of way and areas of natural beauty, to improve public access to the countryside, and to encourage more people to take up rambling as a healthy, recreational activity. It has played an important role in preserving and developing our national footpath network.

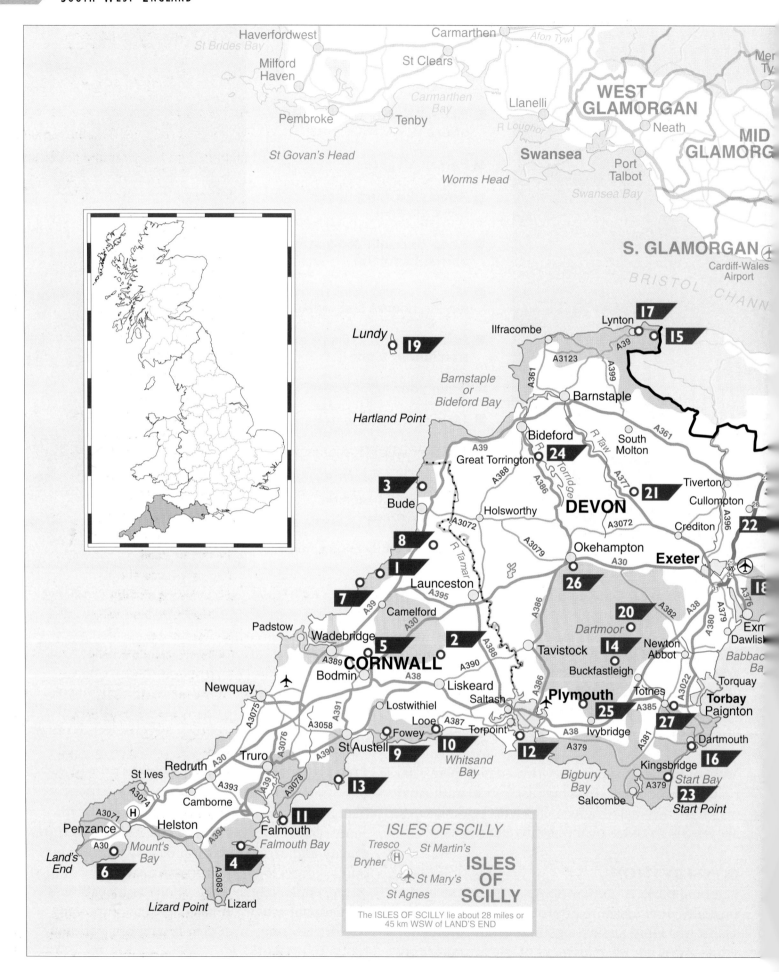

Haverfordwest
St Brides Bay
Milford
Haven
Pembroke
St Govan's Head
Tenby

Carmarthen
St Clears
Afon Tywi
Carmarthen
Bay
R Loughor
Llanelli
Worms Head
Swansea Bay

WEST
GLAMORGAN
Swansea
Neath
Port
Talbot

MER
TY
MID
GLAMORG

S. GLAMORGAN
Cardiff-Wales
Airport
BRISTOL CHANN

Lundy **19**

Ilfracombe
Lynton **17**
A3123
A39
A361
A399
15

Barnstaple
or
Bideford Bay

Hartland Point

Barnstaple
A361
R Taw
South
Molton
Tiverton
Cullompton
A361

A39
Bideford
R
Great Torrington **24**
A388
R Taw
R Torridge
A377
A386
Holsworthy
DEVON
A3072
Crediton
A396
22
21

3
Bude

A3072
R Tamar
A3079
Okehampton
Exeter
A30

8
1
Launceston
A395
26
A386
18

7
A39
Camelford
A30
20
A382
A38
A379
Exm
Dawlis

Padstow
Wadebridge
5
Dartmoor
14
Newton
Abbot
Babbac
Ba

A389
CORNWALL
Bodmin
2
A388
A390
A38
Tavistock
Buckfastleigh
A386
Torquay
A3022
Torbay
Paignton

Newquay
A3075
A391
Liskeard
Saltash
A386
Plymouth
Totnes
A385
27
Dartmouth
16

A3058
Lostwithiel
Looe
A387
Torpoint
25
A38
Ivybridge
A381
Kingsbridge
Start Bay

Truro
A390
A3078
St Austell
9
Fowey
10
12
A379
*Whitsand
Bay*
*Bigbury
Bay*
Salcombe
A379
23
Start Point

Redruth
St Ives
A393
Camborne
13

A3074
A3075
H
Helston
A394
11
Falmouth
Falmouth Bay

Penzance
A30
*Mount's
Bay*
4

*Land's
End*
6

A3083
Lizard Point
Lizard

ISLES OF SCILLY
Tresco   *St Martin's*
Bryher **H**
          ✈ *St Mary's*
St Agnes

**ISLES
OF
SCILLY**

The ISLES OF SCILLY lie about 28 miles or
45 km WSW of LAND'S END

South West England

All the walks featured in this book are plotted and numbered on the regional map (left) and listed in the box below.

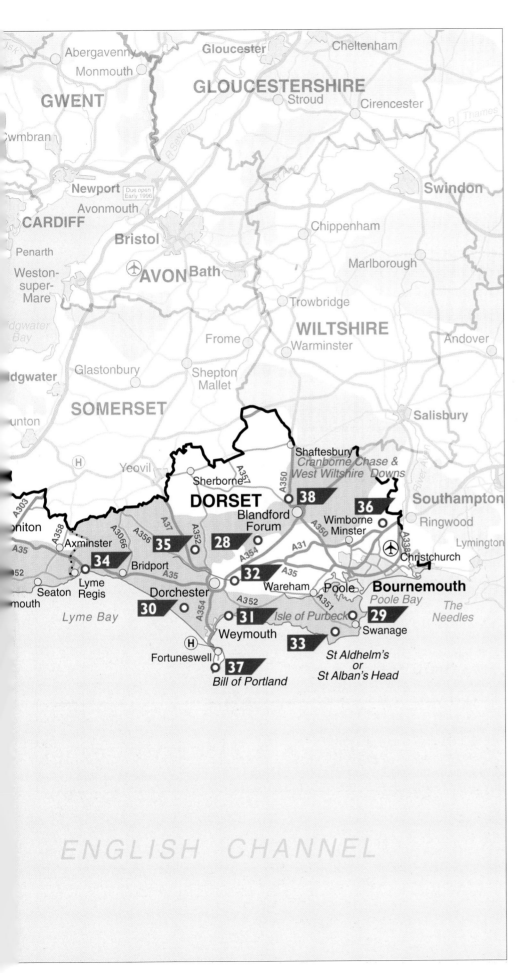

USING MAPS

Although the OUT & ABOUT WALKING GUIDES TO BRITAIN give you all the information you need, it is useful to have some basic map skills. Most of us have some experience of using a motoring atlas to navigate by car. Navigating when walking is much the same, except that mistakes are much more time and energy consuming and, if circumstances conspire, could lead to an accident.

A large-scale map is the answer to identifying where you are. Britain is fortunate in having the best mapping agency in the world, the Ordnance Survey, which produces high-quality maps, the most popular being the 1:50,000 Landranger series. However, the most useful for walkers are the 1:25,000 Pathfinder, Explorer and Outdoor Leisure maps.

THE LIE OF THE LAND

A map provides more than just a bird's eye view of the land; it also conveys information about the terrain – whether marshy, forested, covered with tussocky grass or boulders; it distinguishes between footpaths and bridleways; and shows boundaries such as parish and county boundaries.

Symbols are used to identify a variety of land-marks such as churches, camp and caravan sites, bus, coach and rail stations, castles, caves and historic houses. Perhaps most importantly of all, the shape of the land is indicated by contour lines. Each line represents land at a specific height so it is possible to read the gradient from the spacing of the lines (the closer the spacing, the steeper the hill).

GRID REFERENCES

All Ordnance Survey maps are over-printed with a framework of squares known as the National Grid. This is a reference system which, by breaking the country down into squares, allows you to pinpoint any place in the country and give it a unique reference number; very useful when making rendezvous arrangements. On OS Landranger, Pathfinder and Outdoor Leisure maps it is possible to give a reference to an accuarcy of 100 metres. Grid squares on these maps cover an area of 1 km x 1 km on the ground.

GIVING A GRID REFERENCE

Blenheim Palace in Oxfordshire has a grid reference of **SP 441 161**. This is constructed as follows:

SP These letters identify the 100 km grid square in which Blenheim Palace lies. These squares form the basis of the National Grid. Information on the

100 km square covering a particular map is always given in the map key.

441 161 This six figure reference locates the position of Blenheim Palace to 100 metres in the 100 km grid square.

44 This part of the reference is the number of the grid line which forms the western (left-hand) boundary of the 1 km grid square in which Blenheim Palace appears. This number is printed in the top and bottom margins of the relevant OS map (Pathfinder 1092 in this case).

16 This part of the reference is the number of the grid line which forms the southern (lower) boundary of the 1 km grid square in which Blenheim Palace appears. This number is printed in the left- and right-hand margins of the relevant OS map (Pathfinder 1092).

These two numbers together (SP 4416) locate the bottom left-hand corner of

the 1 km grid square in which Blenheim Palace appears. The remaining figures in the reference **441 161** pinpoint the position within that square by dividing its western boundary lines into tenths and estimating on which imaginary tenths line Blenheim Palace lies.

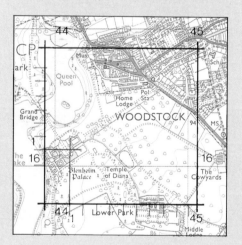

Through the Valency Valley

DEREK PRATT/WATERWAYS PHOTO LIBRARY. INSET HEATHER ANGEL

JOHN WATNEY

▲ *The narrow inlet of Boscastle harbour. (inset) Herring gulls lining up for the catch.*
◄ *A leafy Cornish lane.*

From Boscastle harbour to a Hardy monument

This walk starts and finishes at the picturesque harbour of Boscastle, mouth of the River Valency. Along the way it takes in St Juliot's Church where, as a young man, the writer Thomas Hardy was employed as the architect in charge of its restoration.

For those interested in Hardy, the church is a major attraction of the walk. It was here that he met and fell in love with Emma Gifford, the rector's sister-in-law, who became his first wife.

A VISUAL FEAST

The walk takes you through a wide variety of landscapes, starting in the main street of Boscastle and then turning on to a pathway across a pretty river valley. Next it follows a series of narrow lanes typical of the region, with their high banks filled with flowers. Breaks in the banks give panoramic views over the surrounding countryside. Traffic is light — you often meet more horses along the way than cars. The hills, however, are steep in some places.

At St Juliot's Church, footpaths

FACT FILE

- Boscastle, North Cornwall
- Pathfinder 1325 (SX 08/18), grid reference SX 099913
- miles 0 1 2 3 4 5 6 7 8 9 10 miles / kms 0 1 2 3 4 5 6 7 8 9 10 11 12 13 14 15 kms
- Allow 3½ hours. For short version allow 1½ hours
- Easy on good ground, but steep in places
- P Main car park in Boscastle
- T Bus service from Tintagel to Boscastle
- The town offers a range of cafés, restaurants and pubs
- WC At Boscastle

BOSCASTLE – LESNEWTH – MINSTER WOOD

THE WALK

The walk starts from the main car park in Boscastle.

1 ▸ Walk towards the harbour, cross over the bridge and turn left to walk up the old village road past the Wellington Hotel.

2 ▸ At the top of the hill the road bears round to the left past Boscastle Stores, then right. Here is a viewpoint from what remains of Bottreaux Castle **A**. Just before the crossroads and the junction with the B road out of Boscastle, turn left down the track beside the house called Fairfield.

3 ▸ Cross the little stream by the house called Trebutts, then go through the gate and head slightly uphill through the gap in the field bank to the right. The route ahead is marked by wooden posts carrying circular discs. From the top of the field you have a panoramic view over Boscastle.

4 ▸ At the edge of the field, cross the stone stile and turn left up the road, with high banks studded with wild flowers and a canopy of trees overhead.

5 ▸ At the road junction by the whitewashed house, turn left. Keep straight ahead until you reach Minster Church **B**.

6 ▸ Immediately beyond the church, there is a wooden gate with a National Trust emblem. Those wanting a shorter walk can go through this gate and walk down through Peter's Wood. Cross the bridge across the Valency to rejoin the main walk at stage **14** for the return to Boscastle. The main route continues along the road, at first rising and then, after a short distance, going steeply downhill.

7 ▸ At the top of the next rise, there is a road junction. Continue on the main road to the right, signposted to Lesnewth.

replace the lanes and lead down through grassy fields to the woodland of the Valency valley. A walk beside the gentle River Valency finally brings you back to your starting point at Boscastle.

A SAFE HAVEN

The crooked narrow inlet at Boscastle may seem an unlikely site for a harbour, but it provides the only safe haven along 40 miles (64km) of rocky, North Cornish coast. There has been a port here since Norman times, but the present harbour was rebuilt in 1584 by Sir Richard Grenville, the famous Elizabethan captain who died while in command of *The Revenge* in a battle against the Spanish off the Azores in 1591. It must have taken seamanship of the

Fishermen and their lobster pots on the quay at Boscastle.

S & O MATHEWS

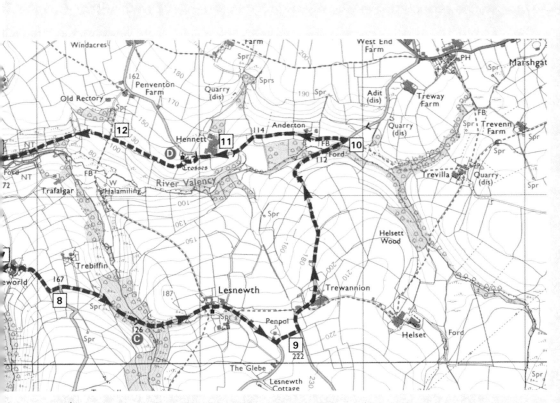

the next field. The path runs steadily downhill keeping close to the hedgerows. After a series of stiles leading from one field to the next, you come to a farm gate.

12 Follow the path signposted to Newmills and go through the kissing gate into the woodland. The rough path continues to head gently downhill until it emerges at the second stone whitewashed cottage to become a broad track.

13 Turn right and immediately left, following the directions shown by the yellow arrows. The path now comes right down through woodland to the bank of the River Valency.

14 The wooden footbridge marks the point where the short cut rejoins the main route. The well-defined path now goes through the valley **E**, staying with the river all the way back to the car park at Boscastle, where the walk started.

8 At the next junction at the top of the hill, keep straight on, passing a small rocky gorge **C**. Go through the hamlet of Lesnewth.

9 Turn left at the next junction past Penpol to a signpost to St Juliot's Church. Turn left down this road.

10 At the bottom of the steep hill, cross the footbridge over the ford and soon after the bridge turn left up the road signposted to St Juliot.

11 At Hennett you will see the tower of St Juliot's Church in front of you, but just before reaching it, turn off the road to the left on to the path marked 'Public Footpath Valency Valley'. The line of the path is marked by yellow arrows. Pass by St Juliot's Church **D**, and cross the stile into

highest order to manoeuvre a big sailing vessel down the inlet, yet even in the last century this was a busy place with ketches and schooners up to 200 tons calling in.

The inlet also boasts a curious natural feature, called the Devil's Bellows, which blows a waterspout horizontally across the harbour mouth for about one hour at either side of low tide.

THE OLD VILLAGE

The village of Boscastle is based on the long street that climbs up the hillside past the site of the Norman castle and which makes up the first stage of the walk. Until 1886, this was the only road to the port. The old houses that line this street are as picturesque as any in the region.

The little River Valency flows through a wooded valley to the sea at Boscastle.

The rough stone walls, often whitewashed, sometimes need buttresses to keep them from collapsing downhill, and age has caused the mellow slate roofs to sag into gentle curves. Much of the area is preserved by the National Trust, and the village as a whole is a Conservation Area.

REMAINS OF A NAME

On the outskirts of the village lies what little remains of Bottreaux Castle **A** . It was built by a Norman family called Botterell and gave its name to the settlement that grew up around it — Boscastle. Today the platform where it once stood makes a splendid viewpoint.

Just before the entrance of St Peter's Wood stands Minster Church **B** . Here there was once a simple hermit's cell, but in the 12th century it became a monastic site. The present building, which was heavily restored in the 1860s, used stone from the early church. It has some notable Tudor monuments with sculptured figures at prayer and some carved slate gravestones.

The roads on this walk are all attractive narrow lanes, but near Lesnewth the scenery becomes quite dramatic **C** . A little stream runs down a rocky gorge surrounded by woodland. In spring, the ground is covered in bluebells.

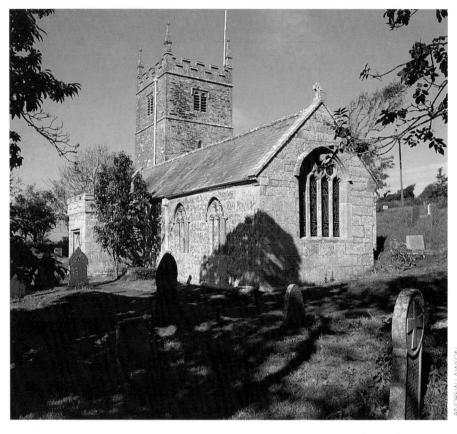

The church of St Juliot **D** at Hennett is interesting not only for its romantic connections, but because it stands as a monument to Hardy's sensibility, for his restoration left it satisfyingly simple with none of the Gothic excesses associated with other Victorian restorers.

St Juliot's Church was rescued from dilapidation by Hardy, who used it as a setting in his novel **A Pair of Blue Eyes**.

After the church, the walk enters the lovely wooded valley of the little River Valency **E** , which runs all the way back to Boscastle.

A Cornish Romance

In 1870, Thomas Hardy, who had trained as an architect, was sent to Cornwall to restore St Juliot's Church. Here he met Emma Lavinia Gifford, the rector's sister-in-law, and fell in love. He was captivated by her vitality, she by his sophistication and literary aspiration. Their courtship was long and idyllic and after the success of his novel *Far from the Madding Crowd* in 1874, they married. But their happiness was short-lived. As Hardy's success grew, he was taken up by society and neglected his wife. Her last years were spent in bitterness. Yet after her death in 1912, Hardy wrote some of his most beautiful poems in memory of her and their time together in Cornwall when they were courting.

MYSTERIES OF THE MOOR

Across the open moorland to see ancient sites and stones

▲ *The Cheesewring is a natural rock formation on the edge of a disused quarry. (inset) The sundew traps tiny insects with its sticky leaves, then absorbs them to gain vital nutrients.*

Bodmin Moor is the site of many mysterious stone circles and strange rock formations. As the walk crosses the open moorland, intriguing evidence of man's past involvement with the area unfolds.

At first this materialises in the form of the prehistoric stone circles, the Hurlers. Later the mining and quarrying relics of relatively recent times provide the interest. The highlight of the walk comes with the ascent to the ancient hill fort of Stowe Hill. Here you can see the famous Cheesewring and enjoy a stunning view across the moor.

A MINING VILLAGE

Minions **A**, on the south-east fringe of Bodmin Moor, was built as a mining township when the nearby Phoenix United Mine blossomed between 1842-98. In its heyday around 500 people worked directly for the mining company and the mine produced an astonishing 83,000 tons of copper and 16,000 tons of tin. Minions is at an altitude of around 1000 feet (300 metres) and it provides an excellent access point to the high moor.

The Hurlers **B** comprise three stone circles, but only two stones remain standing in the southernmost circle. The standing stones are

perfectly sturdy and, despite their Ancient Monument status, no harm will be done by allowing children to clamber on to them. After the

The view east from the village of Minions, showing the engine house of the mine that once provided employment.

FACT FILE
✳ Minions, Bodmin Moor, Cornwall
🗺 Pathfinder 1339 (SX 27/37) grid reference SX 260711
miles 0 1 2 3 4 5 6 7 8 9 10 miles kms 0 1 2 3 4 5 6 7 8 9 10 11 12 13 14 15 kms
◔ Allow 1½ hours
▬ Easy walking, but with small section of steepish ascent. Suitable for young children. Walking shoes are preferable as walk is rocky in parts
Ⓟ Parking in the centre of the village or on the open moor south of the village
🍴 Post office stores and toilets at Minions. The Cheesewring Hotel offers bar meals

THE WALK

MINIONS VILLAGE - STOWE HILL

The centre of Minions village **A** *provides the starting point.*

1 Proceed south along the road through the village until the last of the cottages is passed and open unfenced moor appears on the right.

2 Continue along the road until a track joins the road from the right. A signpost points to the Hurlers. Follow it by turning right up the track until a path leads off to the right. (Although the access track is rather rough, it is possible to park at this point as an alternative to Minions.) The path leads to the three standing stone circles known as the Hurlers **B**. A stone plinth with a plaque inset into the top marks the monument.

3 Walk through the circles to follow the path continuing due north across the moor to Stowe Hill. Rillaton Barrow **C** lies on the highest point of the high ground to the right.

4 As the hill is approached, you will notice an extensive granite quarry. Before the edge of the quarry is reached, a well-defined path comes in from the right. Cross this and follow the path leading beneath the flank of Stowe Hill. Daniel Gumb's Cave **D** can be found over to the right above the south-west corner of the quarry.

5 When the pinnacle of rock known as the Cheesewring **E** stands above, branch to the right directly up the steep flank of the hill, taking a worn but minor path. Reach the Cheesewring after a few minutes of ascent.

6 From the Cheesewring continue to the summit of Stowe Hill **F**. This is reached after first crossing the rubble remains of the granite wall that formed the defensive stronghold of Stowe's Pound **G**.

7 Follow the flat crest of the hill, again passing over the remains of the wall defences that formed Stowe's Pound (there are actually two pounds). Continue to the cairns that mark the northern end of the hill. Return to summit of the hill and continue

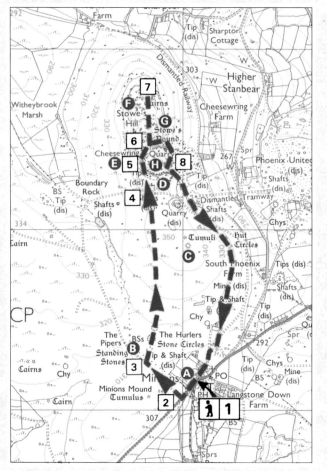

towards the quarry rim to find a path descending the east flank. This path skirts the fenced edge of the quarry.

8 Enter the quarry **H** to look at the impressive tumble of rocks within. Follow the level and easy quarry road south, turning right as Minions is approached to return directly into the centre of the village.

Hurlers, the path then leads on northwards across open moorland directly to Stowe Hill.

Before the fenced edge of the granite quarry is reached, a mound can be seen over to the right. This is Rillaton Barrow **C** and in a stone cist, or tomb, on its eastern end the Rillaton Cup was found. This was made from solid gold and dated from circa 1500 BC – it now rests in the British Museum. Before reaching Stowe Hill, you pass a mine shaft guarded by a rickety fence – keep well clear of it for your safety.

Today this abandoned quarry is used by the Navy to train recruits to abseil the 150-foot (45-metre) walls.

BILL BIRKETT

If you make a detour right, to the ground above the south-west corner of the quarry, you will find the curious Daniel Gumb's Cave **D**. This mystic and 'mountain philosopher', who died in 1776, long before quarrying activities started, built a home for himself and his sizeable family amid the natural granite blocks. The original cave was beneath a 30-foot (9 metre) long granite slab, but what you see now is a reconstruction built around 1870, when the quarry was extended. Gumb was an eccentric stone-cutter who taught himself mathematics, and plainly visible in the roof stone is his carving of Pythagoras's Theorem. Nearby is a section of a doorpost with 'D Gumb, 1735' carved into it.

THE CHEESEWRING

An ascent of 100 feet (30 metres) takes you up Stowe Hill to the Cheesewring **E**. This weird, inversely tapered granite pillar, 25 feet (8 metres) in height and made up of stone rings one on top of the other, seems to defy the natural laws of gravity. It was once thought to have a supernatural origin and was reputedly worshipped by the ancient Druids. In fact, it is a natural for-

mation resulting from the erosion of the softer surrounding rocks. The name 'cheesewring' comes from its similarity to a cider press where a large weight squeezes the juice from the 'cheese' or pulped apples.

During quarrying operations precaution was taken to protect the Cheesewring from toppling when blasting. A stone support was built to underpin the main stem, but if you look carefully you will see the support does not actually touch the rock! In fact, such has been the importance of the Cheesewring that in 1864 an agreement between the Duchy of Cornwall and the quarry masters defined the limits of granite extraction beyond which it was forbidden to quarry. This line was marked by a fleur-de-lis skilfully carved in the rock and this mark can still be seen today right on the edge of the quarry behind the Cheesewring. It is not necessary for you to go beyond the boundary fence to see it.

Progressing from the giant Cheesewring to the summit of Stowe Hill **F** at 1,249 feet (375 metres), you scramble over the remains of a rubble stone wall which formed Stowe's Pound

Stowe Hill boasts the remains of a Bronze Age settlement. Hundreds of these once occupied the bleak granite landscape of Bodmin Moor.

G , the ruined defences of an ancient hillfort, thought to date from the Bronze Age. There are two circular walled defences on the top of the hill: the first smaller one once surrounded the actual summit and the adjoining larger circle protected the rest of the hill. The fine views over the lonely surrounding moors are

The ponies of Bodmin Moor are owned by local farmers but are left to roam and breed wild.

The Hurlers — Standing Stones of Bodmin Moor

The Hurlers consist of three stone circles positioned in a line running from south to north. The larger central circle has a diameter of 140 feet (42 metres) while the smallest circle has a diameter of 108 feet (33 metres). Today the southern circle, reached first on this walk, has only two upright stones remaining and there are many stones now missing. Nevertheless it is an important and impressive site, designated an Ancient Monument. These megaliths are thought to have been built circa 1500 BC and to be early Bronze Age in origin.

According to local superstition, the name Hurlers comes from the ancient Cornish game of hurling, a ball and stick game similar to hockey. It is said that the standing stones were in fact once human hurlers, who broke the rule of the sabbath by playing their game on Sunday. The two isolated standing stones to the west, even though they were not playing, were caught watching. Naturally enough they are now known as the Watchers. While we may never really know what rituals, ceremonies or gods were worshipped here, this remains a special and atmospheric place enhanced by an air of mystery.

The Hurlers were built in the Bronze Age but in pre-Roman times may well have been used as a place of worship and sacrifice by the Druids. (inset) The game of hurling, which gave the stones their name.

Nature Walk

Circles of standing stones (or their remains) and grassed over foundations are evidence of ancient settlements.

exceptional and on a clear day it is possible to see as far as Exmoor, almost 50 miles (80 km) away to the north. To the east you can see past the radio mast on Caradon Hill to High Willhays on Dartmoor, and to the south Plymouth can be seen.

Before descending the east flank of the hill, skirting the fenced edge of the quarry, first walk north along the flat crest of the hill. There are many more fascinating rock formations and markings to be found and the northern extremity of the hill overlooks Witheybrook Marsh and ancient field systems.

The quarry **H** is now derelict, but at its peak in the late 1860s, it employed over 100 men and boys. The beautiful silver-grey granite was sought for its fine architectural qualities. Delivered to Looe by rail, it was then shipped to London and overseas. Westminster Bridge,

Tower Bridge and the Thames Embankment in London are all made from this striking Cornish granite. From here the quarry track, formerly the railway, leads easily back to Minions **A**.

WATCHING WILDLIFE.

The two birds of prey most likely to be seen here are the kestrel and the merlin. On the ground rabbits are common, but you may see a weasel running like lightning across your track. At dusk, which is the most atmospheric time to visit the Hurlers, look out for the elusive red fox. And in the darkening sky at twilight the tiny pipistrelle bat can sometimes be seen.

HERITAGE COAST

◄ *Typical of the North Cornish coast is the rocky beach at Duckpool with the Houndspit cliffs in the distance.*

A walk combining the most attractive elements of Cornish scenery

Duckpool, where the walk begins, is a little rocky bay, which is seen at its most dramatic in rough weather when the waves crash against the cliffs. The first part of the walk follows the long-distance coastal path and begins with a steep climb to the top of the cliffs. The path itself is narrow and rocky, but the effort of climbing is well rewarded by magnificent views along the coast. There is also an intriguing close-up view of the array of vast, white dishes of the satellite tracking station **Ⓐ**.

WINDSWEPT COAST

Beyond this point is an area of coarse grass, gorse and heather, with a large population of stone-chats, swooping very low over the bushes. Field boundaries consist of low stone walls built into earthen banks that are topped by shrubs, stunted and distorted by the wind.

The descent from the cliff-top

▲ *The Spring squill has blue, star-shaped flowers and, like its cousin the Star of Bethlehem, is extremely rare.*

walk is comparatively gentle and leads down to a grassy path beside a stream. The path takes on more and more of the character of a green lane, stony underfoot and running between banks and hedgerows. The upper part of this lane is bordered by dense clusters of blackberry bushes — a paradise in autumn.

TO THE MANOR BORNE

There is a brief interlude of walking down a roadway, but this ends at Stanbury Manor Farm **Ⓑ**. The house itself is easily recognised as an old manor house, with its solid stone walls and massive chimneys. The path leads through the farm grounds, past an ornamental lily pond, to go off through the fields to Eastaway. This too was the site of a manor house, but the old manor has long since been replaced. Here you follow another green lane that soon opens out into a footpath across the fields to Woodford. The village of Eastaway is a mixture of old and new picturesque thatched cottages and sturdy farmhouses.

The footpath now leads across fields before descending a steep path, through dense woodland, to the river valley. This is an area of

ALAN NORTH/NAT. TRUST PHOTO LIBRARY. INSET: JIM BAIN/NHPA

FACT FILE

✳ Coombe, Cornwall, 4 miles (6½ km) north of Bude, just off the A39

▱ Pathfinder 1273 (SS 21/31), grid reference SS 200117

miles 0 1 2 3 4 5 6 7 8 9 10 miles
kms 0 1 2 3 4 5 6 7 8 9 10 11 12 13 14 15 kms

◔ Allow 3 hours

▬ The walk may be muddy in places and the initial climb is steep. Walking shoes are recommended

🅿 There is a car park at Duckpool, on the coast, 3 miles (5 km) north of Bude

R. HILLGROVE/NAT. TRUST PHOTO LIBRARY

▲ *The old mill at Coombe was used for sawing timber grown in the many woods on the Stowe Barton Estate.*

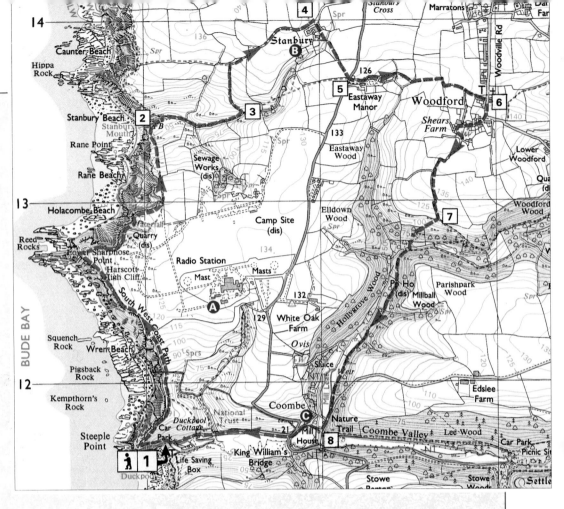

THE WALK

DUCKPOOL – COOMBE

The walk starts at the National Trust car park at Duckpool.

1 Looking out to sea, turn right onto the path leading up to the top of the cliffs. Having reached the top of the climb follow the signs marked 'Coastal Path'. Continue past the satellite tracking station **A** on your right, following the signposts until you arrive at Stanbury Mouth.

2 After descending from the cliffs, cross the footbridge over the stream. Turn right to follow the stream in the direction indicated by the arrow 'Footpath Inland'.

3 Where the path divides, do not cross the stile, but continue on the lane as it swings round to the left. At the top of the lane, turn right onto road.

4 Where the road bends round to the left by the farm buildings, turn right by the name plate 'Stanbury Manor Morlyn Welsh Cobs' **B**. Turn left on to the stony footpath between two ponds. Go through the gate and follow the path round to the right as indicated by the yellow arrow. Head for the stile by the telegraph pole. Continue to follow the yellow arrows.

5 Cross straight ahead over the road and take the path by the sign 'Public Footpath', again waymarked by yellow arrows.

6 At the roadway in Woodford Village, turn right. At the end of the 30 mph zone, the road turns left — continue ahead on the road marked as a dead end and beyond Shears Farm turn right onto the broad track signposted 'Public Footpath'.

7 At the rim of the wooded valley, follow the yellow arrows downhill. The route immediately divides; take the path down to the right. Cross the stream on the footbridge, then cross the stile and turn right. Continue along the well-defined path.

8 At the roadway turn right and continue on the road through Coombe hamlet **C**. At the T-junction turn left, then right onto the road signposted 'Duckpool' and return to the start of the walk.

▲*You can splash through the ford at Coombe or be less adventurous and keep your feet dry by using the footbridge!*

broadleaved wood, dominated by birch, with a smattering of oak and sycamore, and a busy little stream forming an accompaniment to the walk. Soon the valley opens out and reaches the hamlet of Coombe **C**.

GREAT ESTATES

All this area was once part of the great Stowe Barton estate, which belonged to the Grenville family. Its most famous member was Sir Richard, who, as captain of the *Revenge*, fought the Spaniards off the Azores in 1591. The Grenvilles were instrumental in restoring Charles II to the throne and, as a reward, Sir John Grenville was made Earl of Bath. His great house has gone, but the estates survive.

The old water mill, which was used to grind corn and work a saw mill, still stands. For a time Coombe was home to the eccentric Reverend Stephen Hawker of Morwenstow, who stayed in a cottage (Hawker's Cottage) just across the ford. He is best known as the founder of the Harvest Festival service.

Today, much of the area around Coombe is owned by the National Trust, and the hamlet leased by the Landmark Trust. The road passes through a ford, but walkers can keep dry by crossing on the footbridge. For the final section of the walk, the valley broadens out as the river flows down to the sea at Duckpool.

FRENCHMAN'S CREEK

The haunt of smugglers and the setting of a romantic novel

▲ *The Helford River estuary is one of the many remote Cornish creeks that, on a moonless evening, made the perfect haunt for smugglers. A fig tree (left) grows from the wall of the church at the village of Manaccan.*

This walk is centred on the secluded wooded valley of Frenchman's Creek and includes visits to two delightful villages.

Helford **Ⓐ** is a beautiful fishing village, grouped on either bank of a creek that feeds into the Helford River. Stone cottages, some white-washed, others left as rough granite, some thatched and others topped with slate roofs, clamber up the steep hillsides. A wooden footbridge crosses the water next to the ford, beside which is a simple boathouse with a ship weather vane and a fig-urehead set in the gable end.

In summer, a ferry runs across the river from Helford Point. The steep

FACT FILE

⚓ Helford

🗺 Pathfinder 1370 (SW 72/82), grid reference SW 758259

miles 0 — 1 — 2 — 3 — 4 — 5 — 6 — 7 — 8 — 9 — 10 miles
kms 0 — 1 2 3 4 5 6 7 8 9 10 11 12 13 14 15 kms

◔ Allow 2 hours

▭ Easy going on good paths and roadways

🅿 Public car park at Helford

🌐 Public house and toilets at Helford, pub at Manaccan

path gives steadily improving views out over Helford, before levelling out into a lane across the headland.

Frenchman's Creek **Ⓑ** is narrow and secluded, given a secretive air by the woodland that crowds down to the water's edge. It became famous as the setting for Daphne du Maurier's romantic novel of the same name. In the 18th century this was the haunt of smugglers and many of the houses in Helford are said to stand over secret cellars.

The path begins high above the river, passing through a rough land-scape of gorse and bracken with good views of creek and river.

THE WALK

HELFORD – MANACCAN

The walk begins at the car park in Helford **Ⓐ**.

1 Turn right out of the car park onto the road and go down the hill to cross the creek on the wooden footbridge. At the end of the bridge, turn right and follow the road.

2 Turn left up the steep lane beside Well House and follow it uphill.

3 At the T-junction turn right to cross the cattle grid in the direction indicated by the signpost to Frenchman's Creek.

4 Where the track divides, turn left. Just before the gateway and drive marked 'Private' turn left and cross the stile to join the footpath along Frenchman's Creek **Ⓑ**. At the head of the creek, the path follows uphill to the left, joining a broad track coming up from the right. Continue on uphill.

5 At the top of the hill turn right through the gate, then right again at the roadway.

6 At the T-junction turn left. Cross straight over the main road and continue onto the village of Manaccan **Ⓒ**.

7 At the T-junction at the edge of the village, turn left and continue up the hill, past the school. (To visit the pub, turn right at this junction. Then retrace your steps back to the junction.)

8 At the road junction continue straight on towards Helford. At the top of the hill, turn left by the sign 'Public footpath', then turn right onto the path down to Helford. At the road turn left to return to the start.

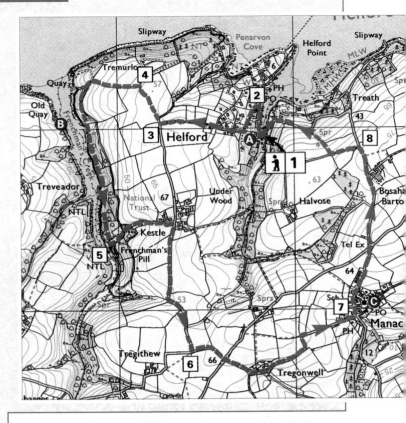

Frenchman's Creek appears at first as a broad inlet, but it steadily narrows and the path soon descends through increasingly dense woodland to the water's edge. Then the creek narrows to little more than a stream, overlooked by a simple fisherman's cottage, recently restored by the Landmark Trust, and the path turns sharply uphill. As the path runs clear of the trees, it emerges into farmland where, in early spring, the fields are crowded with daffodils.

THE PLACE OF MONKS

At the end of the path the route moves onto a typical Cornish lane, narrow and hemmed in by high banks. Where the road swings sharply to the left, it becomes even more constricted and the banks rise up well above head height.

Manaccan itself **Ⓒ** is a tight cluster of buildings, dominated by a rather grand house with a magnificent thatched roof. The village was first mentioned in AD 967 as Lesmanoc, the Place of Monks, but the church itself is later, dating from the 12th century. It has a curious memorial in the north wall to the 'Scientific Parson', the Reverend W. Gregor who, in 1790, discovered a strange black powder. He called this Menachanite, but it is now known as the light, strong metal, titanium.

▲*On a sunny day, Helford Creek is one of the most attractive fishing villages in the country.*

ANDREW BESLEY

AA PICTURE LIBRARY

▲*Many charming cottages in the area have connections with smuggling. Cellars used to bulge with contraband.*

THE CAMEL TRAIL

JONATHAN PLANT. INSET: C. A. HILL/NATURE PHOTOGRAPHERS

Along the route of the old Bodmin and Wadebridge Railway

The hamlet of Helland is little more than a scatter of houses dominated by the granite tower of the parish church. The church seems surprisingly large for such a small place, but it serves a wide community of farms and other hamlets.

From Helland there is a view across to the wooded hills on the opposite side of the Camel Valley. The grey patches among the greenery are tongues of spoil from old quarry workings. The single track road down the hill towards Hellandbridge is typically Cornish with very high banks on either side. The road sinks ever deeper as it goes downhill until the stony banks themselves reach well above head height and are then topped by stunted trees and hedgerows.

Hellandbridge, at the bottom of the hill, is an attractive group of

FACT FILE

- ☀ Helland, 2½ miles (4 km) north of Bodmin
- 🆗 Pathfinder 1338 (SX 07/17), grid reference SX 075710

miles 0 1 2 3 4 5 6 7 8 9 10 miles
kms 0 1 2 3 4 5 6 7 8 9 10 11 12 13 14 15 kms

- ◔ Allow 2 hrs
- ◼ Mostly easy walking with one moderately steep hill. The Camel Trail is also very popular with cyclists
- P In side road by Helland church
- 🍺 Pub at Blisland
- 🍴 Cafés, pubs and toilets in Bodmin

stone cottages. Although the walk now turns onto the disused railway, it is worth walking on a short distance to see the attractive medieval stone bridge across the River Camel Ⓐ. The narrow roadway has passing places created above the massive

▲*The Camel Trail follows the path of the first Cornish passenger steam railway, opened in 1834. The nocturnal tawny owl (inset) swoops silently on small mammals, its main prey.*

supporting piers of the old bridge.

The Camel Trail Ⓑ itself is based on the track bed of the old Bodmin and Wadebridge Railway. Designed by a Cornishman, Henry Taylor, this was the first railway built in Cornwall for the use of steam locomotives, though it was not joined to the rest of the network until 1886.

RIVER VIEW

The trail is named after the River Camel whose valley the old railway line used to follow. It has much the same character as a country lane, with banks and hedgerows on either side. Shortly after joining the walk, look out for one of the old railway distance stones to the right of the path. After leaving the shallow cutting, the path enters woodland and the river, which up to now has only been heard gurgling behind the

THE WALK

HELLAND AND THE RIVER CAMEL

The walk starts by Helland church.

▶ **1** At the T-junction, with the church behind you, turn left and take the road downhill for about ¾ mile (1.2 km).

▶ **2** At the foot of the hill continue on the road as it bends round to the right towards the River Camel **Ⓐ**.

▶ **3** At the railway crossing, turn right onto the Camel Trail **Ⓑ**.

▶ **4** By the signpost to Poley's Bridge, cross the stile by the car park and take the road up through the woods.

▶ **5** About 200 yards (180 metres) before the top of the hill you will see the driveway to Coldrenick on your left, marked by stone gateposts. Opposite this is a very high stone stile signed 'public footpath'. Go over the stile and through the field, with the hedge on your left, to a farm track. Go left, then immediately right and continue in the same direction with the hedge on your right. Make for the gate to the right of the farmhouse across the field to your left. If the stile is overgrown and impassable, continue to the top of the hill and turn right, as signposted, to Helland.

▶ **6** At the roadway, turn right. Pass through Lower Kernick **Ⓒ**, following the road as it bears to the left.

▶ **7** At the T-junction turn right and return to Helland.

BOTH PHOTOS JONATHAN PLANT

trees, comes into view. The track itself runs on a little ledge cut into the rock of the hillside and is overhung by trees. The old railway was built more or less straight, but the river bends and twists, sometimes running alongside the trail then swinging away again.

By the traditional stone farmhouse 'Waterland', there are wider views across the valley to the steep, heavily-wooded slopes on the opposite bank. On the near side of the river, green fields run down to the

◀ *Note the massive supporting pillars of this medieval stone bridge, which spans the River Camel.*

track. Shrubs and trees line the route; elder, beech, birch and dog rose are well established and blackberries grow in profusion. A thin line of oak woodland straddles a small stream, which meets the line just before the path itself enters Shell Wood — an area of mixed pine and broad-leaved woodland. Here the path passes through an avenue of oak while the river rushes through a series of small falls. Look out for the pathside benches which are made out of old railway sleepers.

GLORIOUS BANKS

After leaving the Camel Trail, the walk joins the lane that climbs uphill through the wood, between high banks. These are seen at their best in spring and early summer

▶ *Part of the walk leads through the verdant Camel Valley, which includes Shell Wood.*

when they are a mass of flowers.

Across the fields is Lower Kernick **Ⓒ**, where the farm is built in the typical style of the area, with slate-hung walls. From here, there are particularly good views back across the Camel Valley.

LAMORNA COVE

Crowning the summit of Boscawen Point **E** is an impressive jumble of granite pinnacles and blocks. In the breeding season, a colony of herring gulls will be visible just across the top of the cliff. Down the hill and past the meadow, a glade of stunted oaks offers dappled shade, and next, by contrast, St Loy's Cove **F**, presents an array of giant crystalline rock.

GRANITE MONUMENTS

After passing Boskenna the road leads rapidly to the St Buryan junction. On the right is the distinctive Boskenna Cross **G**. On a widened verge a little further along the road, close inspection of a pile of granite blocks reveals the tomb-like structure of Tregiffian Barrow **H**.

Further on, the Merry Maidens stone circle **J** dates from 2500 to 1500 BC. In the fields beyond, The Pipers **K** are two tall granite standing stones positioned 100 yards (90 metres) apart, said to be the largest standing stones in Cornwall.

ANDREW BESLEY. INSET:W. WISNIEWSKI/FRANK LANE PICTURE AGENCY

▲*Looking west from Boscawen Point, there are breathtaking views across Paynter's and St Loy's Coves. The kittiwake (inset) feeds from the sea surface, or dives underwater for its food.*

Over clifftops and past ancient monuments with stunning seascape views

Lamorna Cove is an ex-fishing quay on one of West Penwith's most delightful sections of coastline. Most of the coastal section of the walk crosses the gentle seaward flanks of the surrounding countryside, occasionally ascending to a stunning viewpoint, but mainly staying sheltered from the full effects of the wind.

The most spectacular view of

Lamorna Cove **A** is from the flat-topped stone quay breakwater and harbour. In front, there is an unbroken view out across the sea. As the path rises up to Lamorna Point, a Celtic-fashioned stone cross **B** can be seen just below it. On the seaward side, an inscription reads something like 'EWW, MAY 13, 1873'. Speculation relates it to the wrecking of the *Garonne* in May 1868, when the bodies of two young girls were washed ashore.

The rocky pinnacled summit of Carn Barges **C** offers an excellent view across to the lighthouse **D** standing above the cliffs of Tater-du.

FACT FILE

* Lamorna, 4 miles (6 km) south of Penzance

* Pathfinder 1368 (SW 32/42), grid reference SW 450240

  miles 0 1 2 3 4 5 6 7 8 9 10 miles
  kms 0 1 2 3 4 5 6 7 8 9 10 11 12 13 14 15 kms

* Allow 3½ hours

* Coastal section includes quite a steep ascent and descent. Muddy section, so walking boots are recommended. Children should be carefully supervised on the coastal path. In summer, sections of the path are overgrown; in wet weather waterproofs are recommended

* **P** Lamorna Cove, at the front of the bay or on the top of the harbour quay

* Café at the harbour. Lamorna Wink Inn

* **WC** At the bay

THE WALK

LAMORNA COVE – LAMORNA

The walk begins on the quay at Lamorna Cove **A**.

1 Walk westwards along the top of the quay wall in Lamorna Cove which leads to the coastal path. Initially scramble through a cluster of granite rocks, and continue to take care until you reach the top of Carn Barges. Continue along the path rising past a Celtic-fashioned stone **B** to the summit of Lamorna Point.

2 The path now dips slightly then levels off to lead towards the next headland of Carn Barges **C**. Timber steps lead up to the summit of the rocky head. A wooden sign points along the coastal path. Continue along the coastal path which zigzags up a hill before reaching the lane above the lighthouse of Tater-du **D**.

3 Continue up the lane to pass through a green metal gate (squeeze stile on the left). Cottages are above the track on the right and another gate is passed. Immediately after this the coastal path bears left off the track.

4 The track descends quickly and at the bottom of the dip a stone and post stile are crossed (beware small stream on far side which is hidden by vegetation) before a small grove of bushes is reached. Wooden boards span the muddiest sections. Pass through a narrow stone gateway to exit left from the grove. The path rises easily at first but then climbs steeply to make an ascent of Boscawen Point **E**. At the top of the head pass through a stone gateway. After exploring the head and taking in the view continue to dip slightly behind a stone wall. Follow this wall for a short distance until an opening on the left takes the path steeply down the hill to a wooden stile crossing a wire fence. Continue down the hill, muddy towards the bottom, until the path levels. The level path now traverses directly above unfenced boulder clay cliffs (not too high but sheer) to enter a meadow, then a glade of trees. The path takes a left turn and descends until suddenly emerging on the boulder beach of St Loy's Cove **F**.

5 Immediately turn right to find the narrow path between the boulder beach and the small cliff below the wood. Pass a garden gate and follow along a stone wall until a sharp right turn is made. The next section follows a stream which in summer is hidden by lush vegetation. Follow along the bank of the stream, across a stone bridge to continue along the opposite bank. A private drive is crossed (wooden signpost marks the coastal path), then the path continues to a wooden stile crossing a post and wire fence. Turn right and ascend 100 yards (90 metres) until the path splits. Bear right (marker post) to cross the stream again via granite blocks. In front is a small white garden gate, bear left here following the garden fence until the path leads through the glade of trees.

6 A small path breaks off right (at right angles) to lead to a surfaced drive in 10 yards (9 metres). Follow this to pass through a grey metal gate. Keep straight on following the lane through an avenue of trees. Pass through the numerous scattered buildings that make up the hamlet of Boskenna, and continue until the B3315 Penzance road is reached.

7 Turn right along the road to pass Boskenna Cross **G** and continue along the road passing Tregiffian Barrow **H** in the verge until a gate and granite stile are reached on the right.

8 Climb the stile and continue straight up the field hill to the Merry Maidens stone circle **J**. From the circle move across to the far corner of the field beyond. A hidden stile (granite with a wooden beam top) leads through the boundary wall on the left. A vague path now leads across the field directly to an electricity pole in the centre of the field. Looking left from here located in fields across the way, the two large standing stones known as The Pipers **K** can be seen. The path continues diagonally across the field to a gap in the wall/bank and this drops steeply to briefly rejoin the B3315 Penzance road.

9 Bear right to find a junction where two lanes join the road. Take the left-hand lane signposted 'cul-de-sac' and Menwinnion Country House for the Elderly. Continue along this, pass a Wesleyan Chapel on the right until you reach the drive leading to Menwinnion. Take the track that descends directly to the surfaced road.

10 Turn right and follow the road, passing the Lamorna Wink Inn, to return to Lamorna Cove and the start of the walk

From a coastal village to castle ruins linked with legend

Tintagel is famous for its connections with the legend of King Arthur. Tintagel Head is a dramatic promontory, protected by unassailable cliffs and bearing the remnants and defences of a once-proud castle — the perfect romantic setting for Camelot. A large tourist industry thrives on the legend.

TENNYSON'S POEMS

Attention was first focused on the area when Turner painted Tintagel Head in 1819. Interest grew in 1842 when Tennyson wrote his poem *Morte d'Arthur* followed by *Idylls of the King*. Interest in the legend reached a peak in the Victorian era when the North Cornwall Railway arrived at Camelford in 1893 to open the area to a large influx of tourists.

There is no real evidence to show that this imposing site has any connection with King Arthur. But there is no doubt that the site was once an important defensive position. This

DEREK FORSS. INSET: PAUL STERRY/NATURE PHOTOGRAPHERS LTD

▲ *Tintagel Castle is the legendary seat of King Arthur, although the building itself is medieval. The large skipper (left) in its characteristic resting pose in sunshine. Tintagel Head (below) is a craggy promontory on which stand the remains of Tintagel Castle.*

FACT FILE

- ✳ Tintagel Head, about 4 miles (7 km) north-west of Camelford

- ▭ Pathfinder 1325 (SX 08/18), grid reference SX 056892

  miles 0 1 2 3 4 5 6 7 8 9 10 miles
  kms 0 1 2 3 4 5 6 7 8 9 10 11 12 13 14 15 kms

- ◖ Allow 2 hours

- ▬ Tracks and footpaths. Some parts are steep and exposed. Best avoided in poor or windy weather, especially with children. Dogs should be kept under close control

- P Car parks in Tintagel

- ▦ Tintagel has pubs and cafés

- ⛫ Tintagel Castle open all year, check opening times. The Old Post Office, Tintagel, open from Easter to the end of October

---

walk not only explores Tintagel Head but also visits a variety of other interesting sites, including some abandoned slate quarry workings. The route takes in some spectacular coastal scenery and provides an ample opportunity to observe the many sea birds that frequent the cliffs.

Tintagel village is generally very busy in the summer months. It is an easy stroll down Church Hill to Tintagel's church ⒶA, dedicated to St Materiana. It is possibly Norman, but unusually the tower rises from its west end. Inside there is a Roman milestone (AD 250) in the south transept and a Norman font and windows. In the churchyard some of the slate headstones are buttressed

by small stones against the strong westerly gales.

The Old Post Office in the centre of the village is a 14th-century house, based on the plan of a medieval manor house. It became a letter-receiving office during

BILL BIRKETT

THE WALK

TINTAGEL — TINTAGEL HEAD

The walk begins at the large car park on the main street of Tintagel.

1 Turn right out of the car park, then cross the road to turn left down Church Hill Road to Tintagel's church **A**.

2 From the church head south down the coast bearing right on a path leading first to the Old Golf Course and then to the Youth Hostel. Continue behind this, descending slightly to Dunderhole Point. From here it is possible to see Gull Point Quarry **B** across Lambhouse Cove

3 Retrace your steps to the Youth Hostel, then follow the coastal path north. Pass Long Grass Quarry **C** in the cliffs below and continue until you can descend to the wooden bridge between Tintagel Head **D** and the mainland. Tintagel Haven forms a naturally protected harbour and the beach may be visited by descending some steps.

4 Pay your dues, cross the bridge and make a steep ascent up the steps to enter a wooden door in the wall of the castle **E**.

5 Continue through the remains of the castle to exit through an arch in the far wall. Pass a hut, then take the track rising to the left. Follow this track to the summit of Tintagel Head. A path descends in a clockwise direction and leads back to the arch in the castle wall. Return to the bridge. Cross it to follow the road back into the village and return to the car park.

Victorian times. Now it has been restored and is owned by the National Trust.

There is a coastal path leading above Glebe Cliff and through the Old Golf Course once owned and supported by the church. Below the Youth Hostel is Gull Point Slate Quarry **B**. This was last worked in the 1920s when men were lowered from the cliff top to work the beds of slate. Lambhouse Quarry and Longhouse Quarry are nearby; both have ceased operating.

Across from the lip of Long Grass Quarry **C** a large cave can be seen, enlarged by the quarrymen. In the fragments of slate, look out for the 'Delabole butterfly', a fossil resembling a Manta Ray. In fact, it is a shellfish that was buried in the mud that formed the slates some 350 million years ago and was subsequently squashed into this shape.

NATURAL HARBOUR

Along the coast, extensive bird life can be observed. Fulmars glide along the tops of the cliffs, where guillemots, razorbills and shags all nest. In summer, common heather and gorse provide wonderful colouring on the tops, while bracken dies to a rusty red in autumn.

On the rocks sea lavender and rock samphire grow. The latter is a fleshy plant with a distinct, tangy, salty taste — it was once a common food and can be eaten either pickled or fresh.

Many sailing vessels used to frequent Tintagel Haven, a naturally protected harbour. Coal was unloaded, slate taken away and the boats 'hobbled' in and out of the haven. This was a procedure whereby the small sail boats were part rowed and part pulled by ropes.

FOOTBRIDGE AND STEPS

Tintagel Castle **E** on Tintagel Head **D** is reached by a hanging footbridge and steeply ascending stone steps. The castle was built in the 12th and 13th centuries. The walls now look extremely precarious, but extensive restoration work is going ahead and the footpaths here are well maintained by the English Heritage Trust.

From the summit of Tintagel Head there are fine views along the coast and a real sense of its defensive position. The idea that this site was once a Celtic monastery is now thought to be incorrect, but it was certainly a pre-Norman trading settlement or chieftain's stronghold. The flat summit is a good location to enjoy the view or a picnic before taking the track back to the castle.

ANDREW BESLEY

◄The Old Post Office in the centre of Tintagel village is a 14th-century stone building with a slate roof and a large hall, in the style of a medieval manor house. It is now owned by the National Trust.

WOODS AND LANES

feet (30m) high. The massive porch originally had a schoolroom above it, and now provides a home for the old village stocks. There is an interesting slate sundial on the wall.

The interior was restored somewhat heavy-handedly by the Victorians but, fortunately, the medieval aisle roofs, with their carved bosses, have survived. Back outside, in the graveyard, are a number of attractively carved slate monuments: look, for example, for the memorial to John Pethick, with its trumpeting angels, in the church wall.

THE COLLEGE

The route goes past The College, a building with a long history. A local shepherdess, Thomasine Bonaventure, caught the eye of a visiting merchant, who married her. In 1508, she purchased land for a school and chantry at her old home, and The College was established. It is now owned by the Landmark Trust, who let it as a holiday home.

Just beyond The College is a green where a whitewashed house

ALEXANDER OLDFIELD. INSET:L.CAMPBELL/NHPA

▲ *A footbridge leads across the moat of a ruined manor. The floor plan can still be made out from the low, grass-covered walls. The delicious penny-bun, or cep, mushroom (left) grows in damp grass. A fine sundial (right) adorns the wall of Week St Mary's church.*

ALEXANDER OLDFIELD

Timeless Cornish countryside near the Devon border

The north-eastern corner of Cornwall, bordered by Bodmin Moor, the Tamar Valley and the sea, is an area of gentle countryside where high-banked lanes wind between remote farms and secluded villages such as Week St Mary, where this walk begins.

The parish church of St Mary **Ⓐ**, near the start of the walk, has a splendid granite tower, almost 100

FACT FILE

✳ Week St Mary, 5½ miles (8.8km) south-east of Bude, off the A39

⊡ Pathfinder 1311 (SX 29/39), grid reference SX 237976

miles 0 1 2 3 4 5 6 7 8 9 10 miles
kms 0 1 2 3 4 5 6 7 8 9 10 11 12 13 14 15 kms

◔ 2 hours

▬ Moderate. Mostly good going on paths and lanes; some steep ascents and descents

ⓅWeek St Mary, by the war memorial

▦ Pub in Week St Mary

---

has a slate-hung wall. The route turns onto a path across the fields to a little footbridge over a stream, and on again with wide views over a gently undulating landscape.

The path ends at a typical Cornish country lane with high hedges. Where there are breaks, there are views on the left down to a deep, wooded valley. The hedgerows are a tangle of plants, with stunted oak,

THE WALK

WEEK ST MARY – PENHALLAM

The walk begins at the war memorial on the green at Week St Mary.

1 Take the road north past the church **A**. At the triangular green, turn left onto the footpath signposted to Waxhill. Follow the path along the line of the hedge to your left to a road.

2 Turn right. Where the road divides, turn left and continue to the foot of the hill at Week Ford. Immediately beyond the bridge, turn left through the wooden gate. Where the track divides immediately beyond the gate, take the track leading uphill to the right and follow it to the road.

3 Turn left, and continue

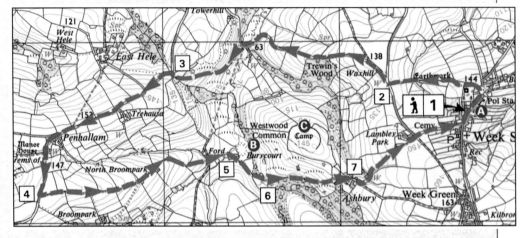

along the road through the hamlet of Penhallam.

4 Turn left onto the track signposted to North Broompark, and keep going beyond the farm, following the line of the hedge to the buildings in the hollow.

5 At Burycourt, pass the house, then turn right

to follow the line of the hedge past the excavated moated manor **B** and along the edge of the woodland.

6 At the post with the yellow waymarker arrows, turn left to take the path through the woods. It goes on uphill past the ramparts of Westwood Common, with the remains

of the ancient camp **C** on your left. The path is waymarked with yellow arrows.

7 The path goes through the farmyard. Beyond it, at the post with four arrows, turn left. At the road, turn right. At the road junction, turn left to return to the starting point of the walk.

---

beech, elder, bramble and gorse all mixed in together. As the road dips downhill, so tall banks rear up on either side, topped by mature trees. The surrounding hills are covered in a mixture of conifer and broad-leaved woodland.

The road crosses a little bridge over a briskly bubbling stream and you turn off to follow a forest path. The rough, broad track runs uphill, leading through dense conifer woodland, speckled with a rich carpet of fungi, before curving round to rejoin the road.

Here, there are wide views of rolling hills out beyond the tall

telecommunication tower to the coast. At this point, the edge of the old woodland is marked by a high bank. The road continues to climb gently between hedgerows. The area is densely populated with pheasants, which strut along the road and through the grassland and crops on either side. The more distant views show a patchwork of small fields, with lanes snaking through them. Where the road swings round to the left at the hamlet of Penhallam, bumps and stones in an orchard are all that remain of an old manor house.

TREE-FILLED HOLLOWS

A little further on, you leave the road for the track to North Broom-park Farm. The view to the south reveals an attractive countryside of hills patched with fields of grain and grassland and broken by hollows filled with trees. Up ahead, beyond Westwood Common, the tower of Week St Mary church

appears as a prominent landmark.

The track comes to an end and the way continues through fields, past a reed-fringed pond, to a little stream crossed at a ford. You go past the barn of Burycourt, and beyond this is the site of an old moated manor **B**. The moat itself is still clearly defined, with two modern footbridges providing access to the remains of the manor itself. This now consists simply of low walls, no more than a few inches high, as if the floor plan were laid out in relief in the grass.

The walk turns into the woodland and crosses a stream at a little rocky cutting. The path then begins to climb uphill past the edge of the woodland, through a straggle of silver birch, to the flank of a hill covered with rough grass and patches of gorse. Here, there are traces of a ring of earthwork defences **C**, marking an ancient fort or camp, probably an Iron Age one. From the top of the hill, there are fine views back over the hills and wooded combes. A broad track then leads down to the road and the outskirts of Week St Mary.

◀ *Burycourt sits at a junction of two stream valleys, next to the site of a ruined, moated manor house.*

ALEXANDER OLDFIELD

CORNWALL

◄*The view down Pont Pill Creek, dotted with sailing craft, to Polruan on the left and St Catherine's Point. The purple hairstreak butterfly (inset) lives in the tops of oak trees along the creek.*

ANDREW BESLEY. INSET: ROBIN BUSH/NATURE PHOTOGRAPHERS

that she wrote her first novel, *The Loving Spirit*.

Leaving the waterside, the walk up Bodinnick Hill passes the Old Ferry Inn Ⓐ. Further up, a plaque on the wall of Hall Walk Cottage shows the way onto the historic Hall Walk, a private promenade created by the Mohun family in the 16th century. Charles I, walking here during the Civil War siege of Fowey, saw one of his men killed by a musket shot fired from across the river.

NOVELIST'S MEMORIAL

At the confluence of the River Fowey and Pont Pill Creek stands a monument Ⓑ to the Cornish writer and scholar, Sir Arthur Quiller-Couch, famous for his novels, in which Fowey is 'Troy', and as the compiler of *The Oxford Book of English Verse*. He became Mayor of Fowey in 1937, and is buried there.

The thick woodland that clothes the slopes of Pont Pill is surprisingly recent. Until 100 years ago, the steep hillsides were grazed, but a change in land management — much of the area is now managed by the National Trust — has resulted in the natural regeneration of oak, ash, beech and sycamore.

The route passes a heronry in the woods and, as you drop down the hill from Hall Walk to the sleepy hamlet of Pont Quay Ⓒ, you may see buzzards and nesting swans. By crossing a wooden footbridge that links the stone quays on either side of the creek and ascending the hill ahead, you come to the door of the lovely church Ⓓ at Lanteglos-by-Fowey. The church is dedicated to the Christian hermit St Wyllow, who, it is thought, was murdered close to the head of the creek, a martyr to his faith. Much of the church dates from the 14th century, though a few Norman fragments survive.

The route loops round on a narrow lane, field paths and a road.

were once owned by the local Mohun family of Hall. Later, rights passed to the Passage House Inn, now the Old Ferry Inn. As you walk down to the ferry, look out for a house called Ferryside beyond the slipway. This was once the home of Daphne du Maurier, and is still owned by the family. It was here

From a novelist's village to fabulous views over the Fowey estuary

Bodinnick village overlooks the estuary of the River Fowey, and the view to its south-west is commanded by the town of Fowey on the opposite bank. Drowned by land-tilt long ago, the river valley forms a natural deep-water, sheltered harbour that is home to countless yachts and part of an important seafaring highway. Nearly two million tons of valuable china clay are shipped out of this estuary each year.

The village owes its existence to the water. Its ferry, formerly a cumbersome rowing boat, was recorded as far back as 1344. A vital commercial link in the old, southern route through Cornwall, the boat conveyed people, livestock and large consignments of beer. Ferry rights

FACT FILE

✳ Bodinnick, 6½ miles (10.4km) east of St Austell

▣ Pathfinder 1354 (SX 05/15), grid reference SX 129523

miles 0 1 2 3 4 5 6 7 8 9 10 miles
kms 0 1 2 3 4 5 6 7 8 9 10 11 12 13 14 15 kms

◔ Allow 3 hours

◼ Mostly good paths. Some short, steep ascents and descents. Muddy in parts in wet weather. Field sown with crops (stage 8) can be wet with rain or dew

Ⓟ Free car park on the left of the approach road to the ferry; look out for a 'Ferry Queue Ahead' sign

Ⓣ Foot and vehicle ferry from Fowey; for details of this and other tourist information,
Ⓘ Tel. (01726) 833616

▦ The Old Ferry Inn, Bodinnick

THE WALK

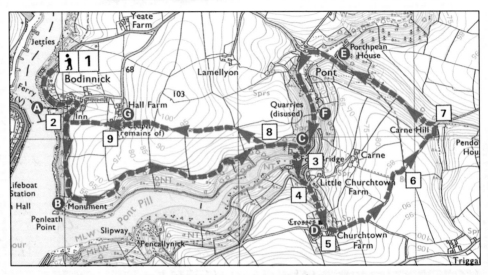

BODINNICK – CARNE HILL

The walk begins at the free public car park just outside Bodinnick on the main approach road to the ferry.

1 Take the road downhill to come to the ferry. Leaving the waterside, turn uphill past the Old Ferry Inn **A**. Further up, a plaque on the side-wall of Hall Walk Cottage marks the way up a narrow footpath to Hall Walk.

2 Continue along the path towards Penleath Point. Here, at the Quiller-Couch monument **B**, bear left alongside Pont Pill Creek until you reach a wooden stile. Cross it and turn right, keeping close to the hedge. When you come to an old slate cattle grid, cross it and follow the path as it swings down to a junction. Take the signposted route right towards Polruan, dropping down to Pont Quay **C**.

3 Cross the creek by means of the wooden footbridge, and take the uphill path next to Pont Creek Cottage. At the top, concrete steps lead onto a small road. Turn left.

4 After a few strides, turn right into a green lane next to Pont Poultry Farm, and continue until you reach a white gate. Enter St Wyllow's churchyard **D**. Turn left through the graveyard near the church door, then left again. Go through the white gate to come out into Saffron Lane just opposite Churchtown Farm.

5 Continue uphill along the green lane for about 300 yards (270m). At a fork, bear left. Where the lane splits again, keep right and continue until the lane peters out into a field.

6 Keep the field hedge to your right to reach a wooden gate. Go through onto a narrow, overgrown path leading to a road.

7 Turn left. After 800 yards (720m) the road crosses a river downstream of Porthpean House **E**. Follow the road signposted 'Pont', passing the remains of an old smithy and limekiln, until you reach Lombard Mill **F**. Fork right, then immediately right again taking the footpath uphill to rejoin Hall Walk and return to the cattle grid.

8 Head diagonally across the field on the other side of the grid (this path is quite easy to miss when crops are growing) and go through the gate in the far left-hand corner. Walk through two fields, keeping the hedge to your right. At the next field, the path crosses to the other side of the hedge and leads down to Hall Farm **G**.

9 Go straight on, leaving the farmyard on your right, into the field. Cross the stone stile at its far side to meet up with the start of Hall Walk. Turn right to return to the start.

▼*This old limekiln at Pont Quay is a reminder of a past industry.*

ANDREW BESLEY

When the road crosses a river, look upstream from the bridge to Porthpean House **E**, once the site of Gragon Leat, which for centuries powered the wheels of a tucking (or fulling) mill. First recorded in 1331, locally spun cloth was cleaned and dressed here until the 18th century, when the mill was converted to paper-making. The settling tanks used in making paper are now covered by the lawns of the house.

More signs of ancient country industry appear further along the road. The remains of a smithy and limekiln, and Lombard Mill **F**, which dates from 1298, tell of a thriving local community long gone.

Climbing out of Pont to rejoin the tail end of Hall Walk, the going gets harder. After bearing right on a footpath by a slate cattle grid, it becomes tougher still, rising to over 300 feet (91m). There are fine panoramic views to all points of the compass. Ahead and a little below, Hall Farm **G** sits on the site of the former Manor of the Mohuns, which was destroyed in the Civil War.

The estate was later bought by Thomas Pitt, grandfather of Prime Minister William Pitt the Elder, but little of the original buildings has survived, save the remains of the 14th-century chapel. Beyond Hall Farm, the path drops steadily down to the start of Hall Walk, then on back to Bodinnick.

Wooded valleys, high hills and clifftop paths around Looe

▲ *The Church of St Tallanus in Talland is a dominant landmark whether it is seen from the rolling hills or the sea. The snakefly (top right) flies in woodland glades from May to July.*

Broadleaved woodland cloaks the valleys of both the East and West Looe Rivers. Their waters join close to Millpool, once a large sheet of water, now a car park, where you enter the thick, green silence of Kilminorth Wood Ⓐ. Many of the trees are relatively young sessile oaks, interspersed with sweet chestnut, beech, birch and the occasional Scots pine. The thin light that filters through the dense, leafy woodland encourages a rich undergrowth.

COLOURFUL PLANTS

In spring, delicate wood anemones and primroses compete for space with ramsons and bluebells, and act as a foil to dark-green dog's mercury. Later in the year, tangles of bramble and wild honeysuckle help to weave the whole fabric of the woodland together.

As you walk by the waterside, look out for kingfishers. Heron and redshank patrol the shallows and

gulls patter in the mud, running on the spot to simulate the sensation of the incoming tide and bring invertebrates to the surface.

Beyond the boatyard, the path is crossed by traces of an ancient earthwork, the Giant's Hedge Ⓑ. Although much of it is no longer visible, excavations have shown that it once ran in a continuous bank 3–6 feet (90cm–1.8m) high for about 9 miles (14.4 km). Legend says it was built by the Devil, archaeologists and historians that it was a defensive boundary built by a local chieftain; its sinuous curve traces a line just below the shoulder of the hillsides.

From the sleepy hamlet of Watergate, you climb slowly out of the woods on a lane. Flowered hedgerows skirt the wood on the steepest section. After the route crosses the main Looe to Polperro road and passes Waylands Farm, the countryside opens out breathtakingly after the tunnelled woodland and high-hedged lanes. Ahead is a welcome descent towards Talland's church, which overlooks a beautiful,

▼ *Saltmarshes flank the channel of the tidal West Looe River as you walk north-west out of the town.*

FACT FILE

✳ West Looe, 9 miles (14.4km) south of Liskeard, on the A387

🗺 Pathfinder 1355 (SX 25/35), grid reference SX 248537

miles 0 — 1 — 2 — 3 — 4 — 5 — 6 — 7 — 8 — 9 — 10 miles
kms 0 — 1 2 3 4 5 6 7 8 9 10 11 12 13 14 15 kms

◔ Allow 4 to 5 hours

▬ Some short, steep ascents and descents. Can be muddy in woodland sections and on the coast paths

🅿 Millpool car park at the start (charge payable)

🍺🍴 Several pubs, cafés and restaurants in West Looe. Seasonal tea-garden in Tencreek and café at Talland

🚻 At Millpool car park and Talland café

33

THE WALK

WEST LOOE – TALLAND BAY

The walk begins at the entrance to Kilminorth Wood Ⓐ, at the western, landward, end of the Millpool car park.

▶ **1** Look for an information board mapping out the wood. Take the tarmac path by the river down to a boatyard. Bypass the yard, following the signpost pointing left up steps. This path curves round and descends steeply to rejoin the woodland walk where it crosses the Giant's Hedge Ⓑ. Continue walking through the wood to Watergate.

▶ **2** Turn left onto a lane between the cottages. Climb steadily past Kilminorth Farm on your right and a complex of holiday cottages just beyond. Bear left with the lane where it meets a farm track, and continue to a main road (the A387).

▶ **3** Cross to the track opposite and slightly right. Follow it past Waylands Farm. Further on, cross a waymarked stile on your right to enter a camping field. Follow the hedge on your right to another stile, at the bottom right of the field. Cross the next field diagonally, aiming for a gate in the corner where some overhead cables cross the hedge.

▶ **4** Go through the gate and head towards the pylon-like landmark tower Ⓒ. Follow the footpath as it turns sharply left, crosses a makeshift stile and drops down steep steps to a lane.

▶ **5** Turn right. Just past Talland Barton Caravan Park, take the path on your left into Talland churchyard Ⓓ. Go through the covered porch; the path descends through the graveyard back to the lane below. Turn left, steeply downhill to the rocky seashore at Talland Bay Ⓔ.

▶ **6** Leave the lane. By Rotterdam Cottage is a parking space; facing the sea, cross a stile to the coast path on your left. Keep to the coast path for about 2¼ miles (3.6km); on the way, you round the Hore Stone, from where there are excellent views of Looe Island Ⓕ.

▶ **7** Pass through a kissing-gate and keep to the seaward side of the road.

Follow a path down steps to the waterfront promenade, and return to the road up concrete steps by the Hannafore Point Hotel. Keep right on the road around the point, and descend steps to a second waterfront walk. Continue along the quay past St Nicholas's Church Ⓖ. Pass under the road-bridge to arrive at the Old Mill Ⓗ. Go ahead past Pearn's Chandlery to return to the Millpool car park.

Nature Walk

As you walk through woodland in springtime, keep a look out for the interesting flowers on the trees.

BEECH flowers open in May. The more numerous male catkins hang down; female catkins stand upright.

HAWTHORN was once widely used in Mayday festivities. Its flowers are fragrant and open in May.

HAZEL trees flower in February and March. Male catkins are much larger than the tiny red female flowers.

▶ *At the hamlet of Watergate there is a climb up to Waylands Farm then a descent to the coast, where you pass the measured nautical mile marks (above).*

intimate cove and bay.

The way is marked by a curious structure on the hill in front. One of four towers overlooking the coast between here and Looe, it is part of a landmark system ⓒ denoting one end of a measured nautical mile. Royal Naval ships from Devonport Dockyard, a little to the east, steam between them, taking timings to check their speed.

SMUGGLERS' CHURCH

Talland's church ⓓ shelters under the landward brow of the coastal hill. Its dedication, to St Tallanus, is unique, and the church stands on or near the site of the saint's cell. Cut into solid rock, the tower is detached from the body of the church but linked to the main door by an outer porch, notable for its wagon roof. The church has old smuggling connections, as has the bay below.

Richard Doidge, a Georgian vicar, was a renowned 'exorcist'. Nightfall frequently witnessed an unholy racket as he chased bands of unruly spirits through the graveyard and

over into the bay below. His actions terrified the godfearing, and only a nerveless man would dare wander uninvited into this lonely graveyard to chance upon the contraband hidden among the stones. Smugglers' graves lie in the yard, and a rhyming epitaph on a headstone just inside the church door refers to a Robert Marks, killed by a single shot fired from a revenue cutter.

The rocky cove at Talland ⓔ has been a smuggler's gateway as recently as 1975. Drug runners

known as the Race Horse Set were caught red-handed by 'Operation Cyril' while trying to land more than 2 tons of cannabis here.

Around Talland's stony beach, the cliffs and rocks biting into the sea are dashed with the pink, green and purple hues of the Dartmouth Slates. You can see these colours repeated in the outcrops by the coast path, which rises steeply east out of Talland back towards Looe.

PLANTS AND BIRDS

The path climbs through thick, yellow-flowered gorse, often 100 feet (30m) or more above the sea. Drifts of thrift can be spotted, clumped on the rocks. At eye level, fulmars wheel in front of the cliffs, alighting occasionally on their precarious nest and roost sites. Kittiwakes, and even the odd peregrine, sweep the cliff front, while behind you, inland, buzzards and ravens appear and disappear over the hills.

The path takes a left turn at a nose of rock called the Hore Stone. Pausing here, you can take in the

◀ *At Talland there is a fine view of the pastures and wooded slopes that rise from the rocky shore along the coast.*

spectacular sea views. Ahead, Looe Island ⑥ (see box) rises like a humpback whale from the sea; to the north-east, beyond Looe, the great sweep of Whitsand Bay curls out to the spur of Rame Head, which hides Plymouth. To the west, the coast views stretch beyond St Austell to Mevagissey Bay and Dodman Point. If the day is clear, an intermittent flashing on the southern horizon will reveal the famous Eddystone Lighthouse, 12 miles (19.2 km) out to sea on a treacherous reef.

ALONG THE FRONT

The walk leads back to West Looe along the seafront and promenades to emerge by the Church of St Nicholas ⑥, the patron saint of sailors, in West Looe Square. St Nicholas's was secularized in the 17th century. It served as a guildhall, and housed a theatre, a school, a market, a prison and even a scold's cage, where hot-tempered women

were held to cool off. It was restored to sacred use in 1852.

West Looe has much less of the holiday bustle of its sister town across the river, and the two are administered separately. There is still a gentle rivalry between the residents, echoed in the local taunt, 'East Looe sunny, West Looe — money!' In season, flotillas of ferry launches take foot passengers between the towns when there is enough water in the tidal harbour.

Along the quay and under the road-bridge is the Old Mill ⑥. Now a café and shop, it was once a tidal mill, grinding first grist and, later, bones for fertilizer. The wheels were turned by seawater trapped behind the millpool wall as the tide went out. The pool would be replenished by each incoming tide. The last fragments of the old wall now form part of the boundary of a small, disused boating lake; the rest is lost beneath the car park.

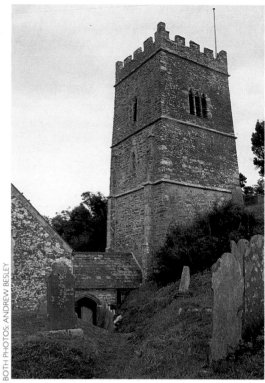

BOTH PHOTOS: ANDREW BESLEY

▲ *The tower of Talland's church was no doubt used by smugglers both as a lookout and as a signalling point.*

A Smugglers' Island

Looe Island is the largest island off the Cornish coast. A shallow, rocky channel separates it from the mainland, and at low tide it is possible to walk half the way out to it from Hannafore Point.

The island has been known by other names, variously St George's, St Nicholas's and St Michael's. At one time, there were remains of a building known as The Chapel on the summit, and a few scattered stones

still lie there today.

A chapel was probably built here prior to 1200 for Glastonbury Abbey, which also owned a small chapel on the mainland near Hannafore. The chapels were served by two or three monks, who rowed between them, and lit beacons and tolled a bell on the island in order to warn passing boats of the fearsome rocks in stormy weather.

Not surprisingly, Looe Island has

Looe Island is wooded at its eastern end, but the prevailing westerly winds prevent trees from growing on the western side.

its smuggling connections. One of the more colourful characters associated with the island in the early 19th century was called 'Black Joan'. She reputedly acted and dressed like a man and was not shy about using her fists. She and her brother, Fyn, ate all the island's rabbits and rats and operated a depot for contraband, charging smugglers a fee for storage. One hiding place for smuggled goods came to light when a restless cow kicked a hole in her shed floor to reveal a cave that led directly down to the sea.

The island is now privately owned by two sisters, Evelyn and Babs Atkins, who bought it in 1964 and have lived there ever since. Apart from their house, a couple of cottages and a jetty, it remains unscarred by commercial enterprise.

Visitors are allowed in season and are free to explore, swim, or watch the abundant birdlife. The sisters' story of how they acquired the island and their life there is celebrated in two books written by Evelyn Atkins, *We Bought an Island* and *Tales from our Cornish Island*.

CORNWALL

A coastal walk around the headlands of the Roseland Peninsula

Unspoilt countryside and spectacular sea views are the hallmarks of this walk around the southern Roseland Peninsula. Roseland owes much of its character to its extreme position on a creek-riven spur of land at the mouth of the Carrick Roads. Its proximity to Falmouth, one of the world's greatest harbours, about a mile (1.6km) over the water to the west, is belied by the area's remote, rural calm.

The walk begins at Porth Farm and soon reaches the sea at Towan Beach, a sandy ribbon above the rocks that appear at low tide. Across Gerrans Bay, beyond the Nare Head to your left, is Gull Rock, an island haven for one of the south coast's largest seabird colonies. The path skirts low cliffs. In summer, crops reach almost to the sea.

FACT FILE

✳	Porth Farm, Bohortha, 8 miles (12.8km) south of Truro, off the A3078
🗺	Pathfinder 1366 (SW83 & parts of SW73 & SW93), grid reference SW 867329

◔	3 hours
▬	Generally easy walking. Mostly fairly gentle ascents, some steep descents by steps
P	Porth Farm car park (National Trust)
T	Passenger ferry from St Mawes to Place Quay, May-Sept; also foot ferry from Falmouth to St Mawes, summer only
🏛	Portscatho, 1½ miles (2.4km) north of the route
🍴	Full range at St Mawes
WC	Porth Farm, St Anthony Head

A wooden lookout post on the path to Killigerran Head is a convenient spot to stop and watch shags or the effortless flight of fulmars. Further on, the bracken-covered cliffs fall away to tiny, inaccessible inlets. From Zone Point **Ⓐ**, the views are truly stunning. To the south and east is open sea; to the west, across the estuary, the dockside cranes and castle of Falmouth; and, to the north-west, the great artery of Carrick Roads probes deep inland.

MIGRANT BUTTERFLIES

Grey seals may be seen here, and kittiwakes heard calling their name. In summer, migrant butterflies, such as painted ladies, may be found among the more familiar species.

A grassy path winds over St Anthony Head **Ⓑ**. A coastal defence site since the Iron Age, more

▲*Looking out across Porth Creek is the attractive, colour-washed Quay Cottage. The cormorant (right) can be seen fishing in these waters.*

recently it has housed an artillery emplacement. The lighthouse, which is open to visitors, was built in 1834. Its lamp helps keep ships clear of The Manacles, an infamous reef 6 miles (9.6km) to the south.

As you walk away north, St Mawes Harbour appears ahead. The open path wends behind the scoop of Molunan Beach, past dramatic groups of pine trees, then drops steadily down to sea level under a canopy of ash and sycamore.

Place House **Ⓒ** stands facing St Mawes, its large gardens running down to the waterside. Sir Samuel Spry built the present house in neo-Gothic style in 1840. The fine 13th-century church of St Anthony-in-Roseland **Ⓓ** is joined to it. This may be because the house occupies the site of an old monastery built, according to legend, to mark the spot where Christ, in the company of his uncle — Joseph of Arimathea,

◀*The route makes use of an ancient stile set in a typical Cornish stone wall.*

THE WALK

PORTH FARM – ST ANTHONY HEAD

Begin at Porth Farm car park. Turn south off the A3078 at Trewithian, signposted

Gerrans, and continue straight ahead through Gerrans and Trewina.

1 Cross the road and take the shingle path signposted to the beach, under the arch on the left of the toilets. Just before the beach, turn right on the coastal path edging the low cliff and follow it past Killigerran Head and Porthmellin Head, all the way to Zone Point **A**.

2 Go through a gap in a stone wall. Continue on the South West Coast Path onto National Trust land at St Anthony Head **B**. Pass the battery on the left. When level with the old military cottages, turn sharp left down some wide steps signposted to the lighthouse.

3 At the bottom, where the main path leads on to the lighthouse, take the small grassy path sharp right. Pass through a gate. Further on, drop left down stone steps to cross a wooden footbridge. Follow the waymarked path alongside a hedge, round the coast to where woods bar the way ahead.

4 Turn right uphill. Cross the stile at the top, keeping to the left of the next field as the path drops to join a track. Turn right, cross an old stone cattle grid and follow the wooded track.

5 Where the track forks, at an entrance to Place House **C**, go right, uphill, on a wide rhododendron drive. Turn left at a derelict stone building and go down steps into St Anthony's **D**. Go through the graveyard and turn left at the exit, on the road signed to Place Quay. Where the road ends, cross the stile on the right and turn left onto the field-edge path. Continue ahead through a kissing-gate into Drawler Plantation and continue on the path hugging the Percuil River estuary. Follow the path as it bears right at North-hill Point and continue to an ivy-clad house, Froe. Keep to the nearside of the dammed lake. Cross a wooden footbridge on your left and turn right onto the path parallel to the road. This emerges at the grassy lower car park of Porth Farm. Head to the far left side and turn left on the road to the main car park.

who traded for tin — took shelter during a storm.

Place Quay could be the start and finish point of the walk in summer, when a foot ferry from St Mawes plies regularly to and fro. St Mawes itself is accessible by ferry from Falmouth. The path follows the estuary of the Percuil River to North-hill Point. The hedgerows are rich with ferns, mosses and flowers. Occasional orchids may be seen and wall pennywort is common.

The final stretch, along the well-wooded Porth Creek, emerges at Froe, a splendid ivy-clad house, fronted by what appears to be a dammed lake. This was a millpool, filled by the rising tide. Beyond Froe the path leads across a footbridge back to Porth Farm.

▶ *At Great Molunan, the path leads past pine trees on the clifftop edge.*

MIKE WILLIAMS

CORNWALL

MIKE WILLIAMS. INSET: NATURE PHOTOGRAPHERS

A Cornish peninsula overlooking Devon's greatest city

From the high ground of Mount Edgcumbe Country Park there are spectacular views over the water to the historic city of Plymouth. Countless vessels, from rowing boats to naval warships, ply the deep channels of Plymouth Sound.

▼*Cannons such as this were trained menacingly over The Narrows from the Blockhouse to deter invaders.*

FACT FILE

✳ Mount Edgcumbe, ½ mile (800m) south-west of Plymouth across the Sound (22 miles [35km] by road), on the B3247

os Pathfinder 1356 (SX 45/55), grid reference SX 452533

miles 0 1 2 3 4 5 6 7 8 9 10 miles
kms 0 1 2 3 4 5 6 7 8 9 10 11 12 13 14 15 kms

◕ Allow 3-3½ hours

▬ Good footpaths and lanes. Some steep ascents and very steep descents

P Free parking at the start

T Foot ferry from Stonehouse, Plymouth

▦ Cremyll and Kingsand

🍴 Café at Mount Edgcumbe, fish and chips at Cawsand, and tea gardens at Friary in season

wc Cremyll, Mount Edgcumbe's orangery, and Kingsand

🏰 / I For opening times of the country park, and other tourist information, Tel. (01742) 264849/227865

MIKE WILLIAMS

▲*From the folly, a romantic ruin, there is a view of Drake's Island, and of Plymouth beyond. Cork oaks like this (right), which has had bark removed, grow in Mount Edgcumbe Park.*

The waterfront hubbub of the city dominates the scene, but never spoils the tranquility of the park.

Mount Edgcumbe Park ❹ covers about 865 acres (350ha). The land came into the ownership of the Edgcumbe family in 1479. The house they built here in 1553 was virtually destroyed by incendiary bombs in World War II. The present building is a faithful replica.

Mount Edgcumbe's great glory, though, is its garden, the oldest landscaped park in Cornwall, and scheduled as a Grade 1 Historic Garden. The garden's finest feature is its trees. There are unusual species, such as Japanese cedar and cork oak, but even common trees, like sycamore, assume a new majesty from their sheer size.

THE WALK

CREMYLL – KINGSAND

The walk begins in the car park just off the B3247 at Cremyll.

1 Turn left down the main road. After 150 yards (135m), turn right through the gated entrance to Mount Edgcumbe Park **A**, then turn left, heading for a castellated building. Go through the arch and past the orangery. Keep left between high hedges to the coastal path. Continue past Blockhouse fort.

2 At the amphitheatre, cross the lawn to regain the path, which ascends into woodland. About 200 yards (180m) on, a folly **B** can be seen on your right. Go through the high gate, ignoring the descending fork to the left. Follow the waymarked path. The next waymark points ahead, but the main path forks right. Follow the waymark to the smaller path to the head of a small stony beach. Beyond the beach, the grass path climbs to join a wider path. Turn left. A fence, marked 'Danger' bars the way ahead, but steps hard right zigzag up the hillside to a gate. Go through. After 20 paces, the path joins a wide track. Turn left and go under an ivy-covered stone arch. Continue on the drive, which cuts inland behind Fort Picklecombe **C**, to the shady Gothic grotto of Picklecombe Seat.

3 Follow the main path back to the coast. After 500 yards (450m), go through two gates down to a stile on your left.

4 Cross the stile, go down two steps and turn right into a lane. A little way down, cross a stile on your left and follow the footpath signed Cawsand for about 1 mile (1.6km) until you reach a gate onto the road at Kingsand **D**.

5 Bear left towards the Rising Sun, then turn sharp right into Lower Row to the junction with Fore Street. Turn right for about 100 yards (90m).

6 Turn right into a steep lane, Earl's Drive. After ¾ mile (1.2km), beyond some farm buildings, turn right, signposted Picklecombe, for 100 yards (90m).

7 Turn left on a path signposted to Maker's church. The path follows a line of telegraph poles. Cross two more fields to emerge opposite Friary Manor. Cross a concrete drive to a narrow path on the left of the house. Cross the stile and keep to the hedge on your left to another stile in the field corner. Cross and follow the hedge on your right to another stile towards Maker's church **E**. At the churchyard wall, turn left, crossing a tarmac drive further on. Follow the signposted footpath over the field to a road.

8 Turn right. About 100 yards (90m) along the road is St Julian's Well **F**. Return up the road and turn right on the narrow path signposted to Lower Anderton and Empacombe. Follow the waymark right and take the lower right path at the next junction. Cross an open field to a gate into a lane.

9 Cross to the stile opposite and continue on the footpath to Empacombe Quay **G**. Follow the edge of the quay past a pink house on the corner to your right. Where the road bears right, go through a gate onto the grassy path straight ahead. Follow the stone wall to a gate opening into a small field. Cross a stile on the other side, and follow the narrow path beside a high wire-netting fence, over another stile and through light woodland. At a junction, bear left along a wide track to a lane. Where it forks, bear right to Cremyll Ferry **H**. Turn right to return to the car park.

▲ *The fine Classical features of the splendid Italian Garden at Mount Edgcumbe were chiselled in 1799.*

A whole day could be spent wandering around the formal gardens, marvelling at the 600 or more species that make up the famous collection of the International Camellia Society, or pondering the problem of clipping the magnificent 17th-century hedge. However, there are other delights to be discovered on the Maker Peninsula.

SEA DEFENCES

The first half of the walk skirts the estate on the coastal path. Beyond the Blockhouse, where a battery of cannons defended the channel through the Sound, is a large natural bowl surrounded by trees and planted with ornamental shrubs. On the far side is the Classical Milton's Temple, named from the inscription it bears from *Paradise Lost*.

Look out for a large conifer with a straight, reddish trunk. This is a coast redwood, which can live for well over 1,000 years and become one of the largest living organisms on earth. This one, despite its size, is still a relative infant.

Beyond the amphitheatre, the path climbs and becomes wilder as it enters the high-fenced deer park. Fallow deer roam the woods, but are rarely seen in summer as they search out secretive places for their fawns. The romantic ruin **B**, just inside the park, was built around 1747.

The woodland becomes richer and thicker between Ravenness and Redding Points. Inland of the path, camellias, eucalyptus, and even large palm trees and mimosa grow.

The protective arc of the quay wall to Fort Picklecombe **C**, which

was built in 1848, can be seen far below as you round Picklecombe Point. The fort, now converted into secluded private flats, was one of a series protecting Plymouth harbour and dockyards. The best view of it is from further along the route.

Gaps in the trees reveal the wooded slopes of Penlee Point, 1 ½ miles (2.4km) away across Cawsand Bay. The woods were planted for game hunting by the Edgcumbe family, early in the 19th century.

Beyond the woodland, you cross the grassy Minadew Brakes, where wild flowers abound. Yellow spires of agrimony, thistles and a pink vetch appear through the tangle of bramble and wild honeysuckle.

Gatekeepers, common blues and speckled woods are among the butterflies abundant here in July.

The midpoint of the walk is at the twin villages of Kingsand and Cawsand **D**. The stream running between them once formed the boundary between Cornwall and Devon. Revisions in 1844 restored the whole peninsula to Cornwall.

MOORLAND VIEWS

Leaving Kingsand, the route climbs steadily past the disused Grenville Battery, and reaches just over 350 feet (110m) close to Maker's church **E**, whose 70-foot (21-metre) tower is clearly visible from land and sea for miles around. There is a view north, following the urban sprawl up the banks of the Tamar, past Devonport Dockyards (see box on page 42), to the Tamar road-bridge and Brunel's railway bridge. On the horizon beyond are the masses of Bodmin Moor and Dartmoor.

A short detour takes you to St Julian's Well **F**, dedicated to the patron saint of ferrymen. The ancient trough fed by a natural spring is right on the roadside, and the restored stone well-house just behind looks like a tiny chapel.

You descend through Pigshill Wood to the muddy creek known as Millbrook Lake, pass the derelict

◄ *On reaching Kingsand, the route turns inland up winding alleys. As you emerge from Pigshill Wood, a lightship may be seen moored in the muddy estuary known as Millbrook Lake (below).*

tower of an old windmill and arrive at Empacombe Quay **G**. It was here that John Rudyerd based his shore workshops for the building of the Eddystone Lighthouse in 1706–09. Rudyerd's achievements were eclipsed by John Smeaton's more famous tower half a century later.

At one time, the quay was the property of the Edgcumbe estate, and the present earl lives in one of the houses here. At low tide, you can see the extensive mudflats, which provide a feeding ground for a wide variety of birds.

A little way round the coast, close to the car park at Cremyll, is an obelisk which was removed from the site of the folly seen earlier. It was supposedly commissioned by a countess to commemorate her pet pig. A lavish memorial to so humble a creature was considered so inappropriate by her heirs that

▲ *This charming pink-washed cottage sits on Empacombe Quay, which is reinforced by stones arranged in a traditional, vertical fashion. Cawsand and Kingsand (below) huddle together.*

Devonport Dockyards

This engraving from the early 18th century shows Mount Edgecumbe in the foreground.

Devonport's story began towards the end of the 16th century, when the westcountryman Sir Walter Raleigh recognized the potential of the site on the Hamoaze.

It was left to William of Orange, 100 years later, to begin the work — perhaps in gratitude to the people of Plymouth, who were among the first to support him in his successful bid for the throne in 1688. It soon became necessary to expand beyond designer Edmund Dummer's original 24-acre (10-ha) site. The influx of workers, formerly housed in ships, necessitated the construction of more permanent housing, and marked the foundation of the town of Plymouth Dockyard. Residents of Plymouth proper were not at all pleased with this bloated infant community; they regarded the dockers very much as riff-raff.

However, in 1824, with royal approval, the dockyard town gained its own identity, as Devonport. By 1837, through relentless development, its population had outstripped that of Plymouth itself.

Still the work continued. The Great Breakwater across Plymouth Sound was started in 1812 and finished in 1840. By the mid-19th century, fears of invasion led Lord Palmerston to order the building of a ring of massive defences around the entrance to the dockyard and harbour. Many of the old forts and batteries remain today.

Devonport's contribution to the local economy continues. Thirteen docks cover more than 330 acres (134ha) along 2½ miles (4km) of waterfront, and employ 15,000 workers, a far cry from the 75 employed in 1691. Its continuing pre-eminence in the naval world now centres on the refitting of nuclear submarines.

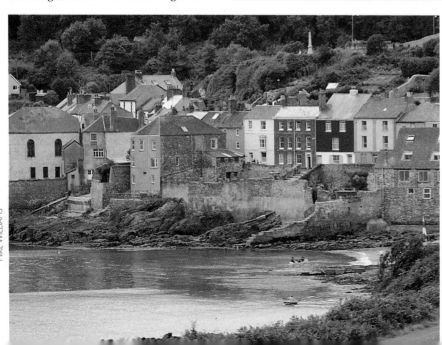

they re-sited it outside the grounds.

The ferry at Cremyll **H** has been an important link to Plymouth for at least 600 years. The site marks the shortest crossing, and in the past was the traditional southern gateway to Cornwall. Centuries ago there was a much larger settlement here, known as West Stonehouse, but it was razed by the marauding French in 1350. The boatyard here dates from the 18th century, and still produces very fine vessels under its modern ownership. Francis Chichester's yacht, *Gypsy Moth IV* was fitted out here prior to his solo round-the-world voyage.

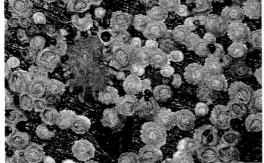

FACT FILE

- ⚹ Gorran Haven, 7 miles (11.2km) south of St Austell

- Pathfinder 1361 (SW 94/SX 04), grid reference SX 010415

miles 0 1 2 3 4 5 6 7 8 9 10 miles
kms 0 1 2 3 4 5 6 7 8 9 10 11 12 13 14 15 kms

- ◔ Allow at least 3½ hours

- Surfaced lanes and well maintained paths throughout, but some strenuous ascents and descents and clifftop paths make it unsuitable for small children

- P Car park at the start (charge payable in season)

- A pub at Gorran Haven; cafés there and at Caerhays in the summer season only

A walk on country lanes and along a thrilling clifftop path

This walk to the wild headland of the Dodman takes in some of the finest coastal scenery in southern Britain, but it begins in very different surroundings, the modern housing of the sleepy village of Gorran Haven.

It takes a while to leave the newer sprawl behind, but once you are on the path to the smaller settlement of Gorran Churchtown, reminders of the present begin to slip away.

As you cross the table-top landscape towards Treveor, you will see that many of the old stone stiles are topped with curious granite columns laid on their sides. These

are the remains of old field rollers.

The walking is easy here, and remains so to beyond Tregavarras, but the appearance of Caerhays Castle Ⓐ, which is splendidly set on a wooded hillside at the head of a tiny sandy cove, heralds a change.

PAPER ROOF

The castle owes its neo-Gothic look to John Nash, who converted it on behalf of the Trevanion family. Nash remains best known for redesigning Buckingham Palace, and for his imposing curved terraces in London's Regent Street. Oddly, he chose papier-mâché as the roof

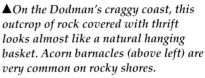

▲ On the Dodman's craggy coast, this outcrop of rock covered with thrift looks almost like a natural hanging basket. Acorn barnacles (above left) are very common on rocky shores.

covering for Caerhays, defying the Cornish climate to do its worst; it did, and the castle was abandoned to the ducks. In 1852, it was bought and restored by a Michael Williams, whose descendants still live there.

Away from Caerhays, the coast path starts to rise steeply. More than 130 steps climb high over Black Rock, giving spectacular views. On a clear day, the huge radio dishes of

THE WALK

GORRAN HAVEN – DODMAN POINT

The walk starts from Gorran Haven's main car park.

1. Turn right onto the road and follow it for about ½ mile (800m), to the edge of the village. Turn left on a footpath by a bench, signposted to Gorran (Churchtown). Cross a stone stile and head diagonally across the field to a gap in the far hedge. Head for the left of a white house and cross a stone stile onto a road.

2. Turn left. Where another road joins, keep right, down through Gorran Churchtown. Go through the village. Just beyond the post office, turn left on the footpath to Treveor. Climb the stile a few strides along, and cross two fields, keeping the hedge on your right. Cross a small lane and follow the path opposite, signposted to Treveor. By a clump of trees on the far side of the field, climb a stile into a road.

3. Turn left, then soon right. Continue past Treveor Farm, ignoring footpaths signposted to Boswinger and Rescassa. Where the road bends to the right, turn left over a stile signposted to Tregavarras. Keep the group of cottages ahead to your right. Cross a footbridge, then a stile. Follow the path through a field, skirting cottage gardens on your right, to another stile at a field gate. Follow the cottage access track, then continue ahead on the road.

4. Where the road bends sharp left, turn right by a cottage on a footpath marked 'Caerhays'. Follow a short track and climb a stile into an open grassy field. Caerhays Castle **A** appears ahead. For a closer look at the castle, and for the beach, toilets, etc, head for the gate in the very bottom left corner of the field. Otherwise, head in the same direction but veer left before the bottom to cross a stile next to a gate, on the left of the field.

5. Follow the coast path ahead, over a stile up steps. You pass Greeb Point **B**, then finally drop to the road at Hemmick beach.

6. Turn right onto the road. After 30 paces or so turn right over a stile to rejoin the coast path. After a gate, turn right and continue to a crossing of footpaths at the summit of Dodman Point.

7. Turn right to the Stone Cross **C**. Retrace your steps, then follow the grassy path ahead. After about 50 paces, the Dodman Watch House **D** appears on your right. Keep ahead to a stile. Cross into a large field.

Keep left, alongside a wire fence. Where this runs into a hedge, look left to see a medieval strip field **E** next to the path. Continue, to a gate in the far left corner. To your left, and slightly behind, is a Bronze Age barrow. Through the gate the path narrows between stone hedges to a junction. Turn right, then right again over a stile, towards the coast path. The high bank to your right is the boundary earthwork **F** of an Iron Age fort. About 50 paces further on is a signposted junction.

8. Turn sharp left onto the coastal route. Eventually, you go down steps into Gorran Haven's Foxhole Lane. At the T-junction, turn left to return to the car park.

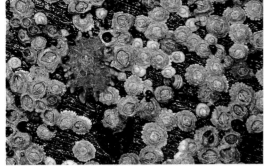

FACT FILE

- ☀ Gorran Haven, 7 miles (11.2km) south of St Austell

- 🗺 Pathfinder 1361 (SW 94/SX 04), grid reference SX 010415

  miles 0 1 2 3 4 5 6 7 8 9 10 miles
  kms 0 1 2 3 4 5 6 7 8 9 10 11 12 13 14 15 kms

- ◔ Allow at least 3½ hours

- ⬭ Surfaced lanes and well maintained paths throughout, but some strenuous ascents and descents and clifftop paths make it unsuitable for small children

- P Car park at the start (charge payable in season)

- 🍴 A pub at Gorran Haven; cafés there and at Caerhays in the summer season only

A walk on country lanes and along a thrilling clifftop path

▲*On the Dodman's craggy coast, this outcrop of rock covered with thrift looks almost like a natural hanging basket. Acorn barnacles (above left) are very common on rocky shores.*

This walk to the wild headland of the Dodman takes in some of the finest coastal scenery in southern Britain, but it begins in very different surroundings, the modern housing of the sleepy village of Gorran Haven.

It takes a while to leave the newer sprawl behind, but once you are on the path to the smaller settlement of Gorran Churchtown, reminders of the present begin to slip away.

As you cross the table-top landscape towards Treveor, you will see that many of the old stone stiles are topped with curious granite columns laid on their sides. These are the remains of old field rollers.

The walking is easy here, and remains so to beyond Tregavarras, but the appearance of Caerhays Castle Ⓐ, which is splendidly set on a wooded hillside at the head of a tiny sandy cove, heralds a change.

PAPER ROOF

The castle owes its neo-Gothic look to John Nash, who converted it on behalf of the Trevanion family. Nash remains best known for redesigning Buckingham Palace, and for his imposing curved terraces in London's Regent Street. Oddly, he chose papier-mâché as the roof covering for Caerhays, defying the Cornish climate to do its worst; it did, and the castle was abandoned to the ducks. In 1852, it was bought and restored by a Michael Williams, whose descendants still live there.

Away from Caerhays, the coast path starts to rise steeply. More than 130 steps climb high over Black Rock, giving spectacular views. On a clear day, the huge radio dishes of

SOUTH WEST ENGLAND

THE WALK

GORRAN HAVEN – DODMAN POINT

The walk starts from Gorran Haven's main car park.

1 Turn right onto the road and follow it for about ½ mile (800m), to the edge of the village. Turn left on a footpath by a bench, signposted to Gorran (Churchtown). Cross a stone stile and head diagonally across the field to a gap in the far hedge. Head for the left of a white house and cross a stone stile onto a road.

2 Turn left. Where another road joins, keep right, down through Gorran Churchtown. Go through the village. Just beyond the post office, turn left on the footpath to Treveor. Climb the stile a few strides along, and cross two fields, keeping the hedge on your right. Cross a small lane and follow the path opposite, signposted to Treveor. By a clump of trees on the far side of the field, climb a stile into a road.

3 Turn left, then soon right. Continue past Treveor Farm, ignoring footpaths signposted to Boswinger and Rescassa. Where the road bends to the right, turn left over a stile signposted to Tregavarras. Keep the group of cottages ahead to your right. Cross a footbridge, then a stile. Follow the path through a field, skirting cottage gardens on your right, to another stile at a field gate. Follow the cottage access track, then continue ahead on the road.

4 Where the road bends sharp left, turn right by a cottage on a footpath marked 'Caerhays'. Follow a short track and climb a stile into an open grassy field. Caerhays Castle **A** appears ahead. For a closer look at the castle, and for the beach, toilets, etc, head for the gate in the very bottom left corner of the field. Otherwise, head in the same direction but veer left before the bottom to cross a stile next to a gate, on the left of the field.

5 Follow the coast path ahead, over a stile up steps. You pass Greeb Point **B**, then finally drop to the road at Hemmick beach.

6 Turn right onto the road. After 30 paces or so turn right over a stile to rejoin the coast path. After a gate, turn right and continue to a crossing of footpaths at the summit of Dodman Point.

7 Turn right to the Stone Cross **C**. Retrace your steps, then follow the grassy path ahead. After about 50 paces, the Dodman Watch House **D** appears on your right. Keep ahead to a stile. Cross into a large field.

Keep left, alongside a wire fence. Where this runs into a hedge, look left to see a medieval strip field **E** next to the path. Continue, to a gate in the far left corner. To your left, and slightly behind, is a Bronze Age barrow. Through the gate the path narrows between stone hedges to a junction. Turn right, then right again over a stile, towards the coast path. The high bank to your right is the boundary earthwork **F** of an Iron Age fort. About 50 paces further on is a signposted junction.

8 Turn sharp left onto the coastal route. Eventually, you go down steps into Gorran Haven's Foxhole Lane. At the T-junction, turn left to return to the car park.

◄*As you walk downhill from Tregavarras, a view of Caerhays Castle opens out before you. From Greeb Point, you can see the danger Lambsowden Cove (below) can present to shipping.*

Goonhilly Downs are visible beyond Gull Rock, over 20 miles (32km) away on the Lizard peninsula.

The National Trust owns substantial stretches of the local coastline, including the Dodman itself. The first section to be encountered is Lambsowden Cove, on the way towards the unmistakable, jagged outline of Greeb Point **ⓑ**.

BRANDY GALORE

Veryan Bay as a whole has long had a notorious reputation among sailors – almost every headland, it seems, has been the scene of a maritime catastrophe. In 1838, the brig *Brandywine* struck the rocks at Greeb Point with great loss of life. Its cargo, hundreds of barrels of brandy, was washed ashore, and the ensuing race between the locals and the authorities to salvage the contraband was won by the Revenue Men.

The path undulates between stunted sycamore, hawthorn and elder. Blackthorn thickets often provide a welcome boundary against the steeper cliff edges. Sea spleenwort can be found in the area, and the rare narrow-leaved everlasting pea is known to occur. Great black-backed gulls, marauders of the seabird colonies on Gull Rock, sometimes sweep by. In winter, there may be the occasional refugee black-throated or great northern diver in the bay.

As you walk above Hemmick

Beach, the grandeur of the Dodman begins to show as the headland bulks before you. From here, the path rises fairly severely — in parts, as steeply as it is possible to walk without scrambling.

COMMANDING VIEWS

Further on, the gradient eases a little, but the ascent is generally relentless. At the top, you stand 374 feet (114m) above the sea. From here, you can see how the Dodman commands the eastern end of the great scoop of Veryan Bay. To the west there are views to the Lizard peninsula; to the east, Looe Island can be picked out against a sweep of coast stretching as far as Rame Head, near Plymouth.

The dizzying height is felt most strongly at the Stone Cross **ⓒ**, where the cliffs fall away to the crashing sea. The original cross was cut from a huge chunk of granite, and erected

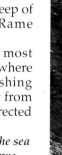

◄*Where the route heads towards the sea over pasture, there are splendid views along the coastline of Veryan Bay. Waves pounding the Dodman have caused sea stacks to form (right).*

in 1896 by the rector of St Michael's Caerhays as a navigational aid. Such is the prominence of its position that it was soon struck by lightning and shattered; it has since been repaired.

Just a little way inland from the cross, a tiny watchhouse **ⓓ** stands close to the path. Now restored as a

Dangerous Dodman

In The Shipwreck *JMW Turner captures the moments of fear that many sailors have experienced around the Dodman.*

Projecting headlands, treacherous rocks, submerged reefs, powerful tidal currents and foul weather driving hard from the south-west have long conspired to make the southern coast of Cornwall an internationally feared hazard for all types of shipping.

The freakishly rough waters around the Dodman — locally nicknamed 'deadman'— have claimed many vessels and lives over the centuries. Ships driven north-east by storms past the entrance to Carrick Roads and the shelter of Falmouth's great natural harbour can find it very hard to escape from Veryan Bay.

In the early 1830s, three foreign vessels were lost in the bay in one storm alone and the terrifying speed with which they were smashed and broken up focused national attention on the problems of sea rescue.

At the end of the 19th century, two naval destroyers, *Lynx* and *Thrasher*, struck the Dodman in thick fog, just below the Stone Cross. Though both ships survived, several sailors died in the incident.

Mystery still surrounds the loss of a 45-foot (14-m) pleasure cruiser, *Darlwin*, in the early 1960s. In worsening summer weather, the craft disappeared off the Dodman while returning to Mylor, near Falmouth, following a day trip to Fowey. After an intensive search lasting several days, only a few bodies and slight traces of the *Darlwin* were discovered; its main bulk and most of the 31 people on board were never found.

next to the 'house' once supported a telescope mount.

As the path opens out into a large grassy field, it passes close to a long, narrow field **ⓔ** bounded by stone walls. This is a survivor of the medieval strip field system of arable farming, and is one of many that once existed here.

The Dodman has a long history of settlement. With the sea as an ally and only one defensive line to maintain, Bronze and Iron Age settlers found the headland attractive, despite its exposure to the elements. The great bank across the neck of the headland, known as the Bulwark **ⓕ**, defines the site of an ancient fort. The Bulwark is not easy to pick out as you walk inland from the cross; its 2,000-feet (610-m) length is better appreciated from the air or the track from the hamlet of Penare.

BURIED TREASURE

However, where the path passes through it, part of the 20-foot-high (6-metre) banking fronted by a ditch can clearly be seen. Two Bronze Age barrows lie within the Bulwark's enclosure. One, close to the passage through the Bulwark, appears only as a very shallow hump fronted by a stone wall, but it has never been excavated and may be brimming with ancient bones and artefacts.

Vault Beach marks the path's curving descent from the Dodman to almost sea level. The home stretch, though, along the cliffs dotted with heather, thrift and ox-eye daisies, climbs again. Finally, the small harbour wall of Gorran appears below to your left, as the path drops towards the sheltered beach and the old cottages of this once thriving fishing village.

▼ *Beyond the Bulwark, the route rejoins the shore and follows the cliff above Vault Beach. After a walk through rugged coastal scenery, the well named Gorran Haven (left) is a welcome sight.*

shelter for walkers, it was once one of a chain of flag signalling stations set up by the Admiralty in the late 18th century. The flagpole fell in a storm, but its anchoring shackles can still be found in nearby rocks. The rusty iron bar in the low turret

JOHN HESELTINE. (INSET) LAURIE CAMPBELL/NHPA

A view of the Dart Valley from Bench Tor

The walk begins and ends on gentle moorland slopes, the remnants of an ancient valley of an ancestor of the River Dart. From Bench Tor, perched on a wooded hill, the view suddenly opens out to take in the marvellous deep Dart gorge. Then it is back through woods and open moorland, with its heather, gorse and bracken, to yet another habitat (this time man-made) – the Venford Reservoir.

DARTMOOR'S ORIGINS

The wild landscape of Dartmoor was created 290 million years ago when a volcanic eruption forced molten granite into the overlying soft rock. Erosion gradually exposed the hard granite, and alternate freezing and thawing broke up the granite to form the strangely shaped tors which are so typical of Dartmoor. Around the base of the tors lie the debris of fallen rock

DARTMOOR NATIONAL PARK AUTHORITY

known as 'clitter'. The name 'tor' comes from *twr*, the Celtic word for tower, which well describes their presence on the moor.

Bench Tor **A** is a series of slabbed granite outcrops, about ½ mile (800 metres) long, at the edge of the moor and on top of a steep wooded slope dropping 500 feet (150 metres) to the modern River Dart **B** below.

From the southern end of the Tor, the most breathtaking view of the

▲ *The view west from the top of Bench Tor. (inset) Bog asphodel likes to grow on marshy moorland and mountains.*
◄ *Part of a herd of Dartmoor ponies grazing near the Venford Reservoir.*

FACT FILE

- Holne Moor, Dartmoor National Park, Devon

- Outdoor Leisure Map 28, grid reference SX 688708

  miles 0 1 2 3 4 5 6 7 8 9 10 miles
  kms 0 1 2 3 4 5 6 7 8 9 10 11 12 13 14 15 kms

- Allow 2 hours

- Easy walking, some avoidable damp bits of moorland, one stony stretch of track. Pipe track slippery in wet weather

- **P** Either side of Venford Reservoir

- Café in Holne. Pubs in Holne and Hexworthy

- **WC** In the western car park of Venford Reservoir

THE WALK

BENCH TOR

The walk begins in the car park east of Venford Reservoir on the road from Holne to Hexworthy.

▶ Walk out of the car park at right angles to the road and gradually move up slope until you come to the leat — a narrow channel carrying water to the Stoke farms nearby. Follow it to the left.

2 At the point where the leat turns abruptly through a right angle towards a stone wall on its far side, the blocks of Bench Tor **A** are straight in front of you. Make directly for the third one from the right. From its summit you look down the canopy of the woods to the white-water Dart **B** . For more dramatic views, walk briefly northwards.

3 Move off the Tor by partially retracing your steps

to the stone wall and then follow it to the left. About ¼ mile (400 metres) from Bench Tor, you meet a grassy track. To identify this exact spot, look out for a pile of granite stones on the left and, to the right, a line of trees forming a field boundary on the far side of the stone wall. This track is a pipe track which carries beneath it water from the reservoir towards Torbay. Walking is easy except on the steepest slope where loose granite litters the path for a while. Continue into the wood.

4 Continue along the path which, after a time, emerges from the wood **C** . Walk along it until you are nearly at the iron railings round the conifer-planted grounds by the dam **D** .

5 Go up the slope to the left, at first keeping close to the iron railings. The car

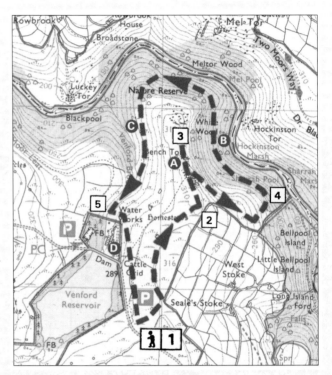

park where the walk started is less than ½ mile (800 metres) away. If you wish to extend the walk and make a circuit of the reservoir for

another hour, go through the gate near the cattle grid on the road which leads to the car park west of the reservoir.

Dart gorge can be seen. Bench Tor, perched on the side of a valley, is a good example of how tors are formed. Because of its situation, erosion is most effective and gravity allows the eroded boulders to fall away very easily.

'Dart' comes from an ancient British word meaning 'oak', and below Bench Tor lies a dense oak wood, coppiced for centuries for its bark (to help in tanning leather), and for firewood and charcoal. Here redstarts and pied flycatchers sing in

early summer and wood warblers trill close to the path.

Up the tributary valley of the Venford Brook **C** , oaks give way to birch, rowan and sallow under which dippers and grey wagtails find good feeding. The dam **D** , built in the 1930s, is masked by tall larches, pines and spruces. Coal tits and siskins revel in this different habitat, and the little reservoir, with its narrow plantation, provides an artificial oasis for wildlife in the midst of a moorland 'desert'.

M J THOMAS/FRANK LANE PICTURE AGENCY

▲ *Pied flycatchers inhabit the oak wood below Bench Tor, where the tree stumps provide good nesting places.*
◀ *The view of the Dart valley from White Wood just under Bench Tor. Across the valley is Meltor Wood. (far left) The granite outcrop of Bench Tor, formed by aeons of erosion.*

JOHN HESELTINE

FACT FILE

- Malmsmead, 5 miles (8 km) east of Lynton, Devon, just off the A39

- Pathfinder 1214 (SS 64/74), grid reference SS 791477

miles 0 1 2 3 4 5 6 7 8 9 10 miles
kms 0 1 2 3 4 5 6 7 8 9 10 11 12 13 14 15 kms

- Allow 3 hours

- Easy walking in the valley but stony in places. The rocks by the river can be slippery in frosty weather. The area is prone to sudden mists in winter. Not suitable for young children. Good footwear with ankle support is essential

- P There is a large car park just north of the road junction

- Light refreshments and toilets at Malmsmead. In summer, teas available at Cloud Farm

Following in the footsteps of the lawless Doone family

This walk will appeal to all those who want to hunt out the secret valley where the villainous Doone family of Richard Doddridge Blackmore's celebrated novel, *Lorna Doone*, lived. It is, however, an enjoyable walk in its own right, starting in a gentle river valley, then climbing up to the open expanses of Exmoor, with wide vistas across the bare landscape and over to the rugged Devon coast.

The route begins at Malmsmead. Here, beside the ford, is Lorna Doone Farm Ⓐ, which could have served as a model not for the Doones' but for the Ridds' farm (see page 52). The first part is on a quiet country road, which soon gives way to a rough bridleway. At first the route takes you along the

▲ *Looking down on the hamlet of Malmsmead from the hills of Exmoor. (inset) The blue tit is found wherever there are trees, from gardens to woods, and lives chiefly on insects.*
▼ *The ford and bridge at Malmsmead.*

flank of the valley with high banks on either side. Where gaps appear, there are views down to the busy stream of Badgworthy Water, with

THE WALK

MALMSMEAD - BADGWORTHY WATER

The walk starts in the car park at Malmsmead.

1 Turn left out of the car park and continue past Lorna Doone Farm **A** on the road signposted 'Public Bridleway to Doone Valley', ignoring sign saying 'Short cut to Doone Valley'.

2 Where the road turns sharply to the right, continue straight on through the gate and along the path signposted 'Public Bridleway to Doone Valley'. The route is marked with yellow waymark signs. Beyond the footbridge to Cloud Farm is the memorial stone to R.D. Blackmore **B**.

3 At Lank Combe stream a short diversion may be made to visit Blackmore's 'Water Slide' - three slabs of rock one above the other where the water slides over them. Return to the path and cross over the footbridge.

4 At a clearing in the woodland, a footbridge carries the path across the river. Do not cross the bridge but continue following the narrow path along the same side of the river.

5 The path begins to diverge from Badgworthy Water and reaches a flattened area, the site of a medieval village **C**. What appears to be the main path crosses the stream that cuts across the route. Do not cross the stream but turn off to the right to climb the hill. The path is indistinct here, but if you keep the little valley of Hoccombe Combe to the left, the path will arrive at a fence to join a broad and clear path. Continue along this path to

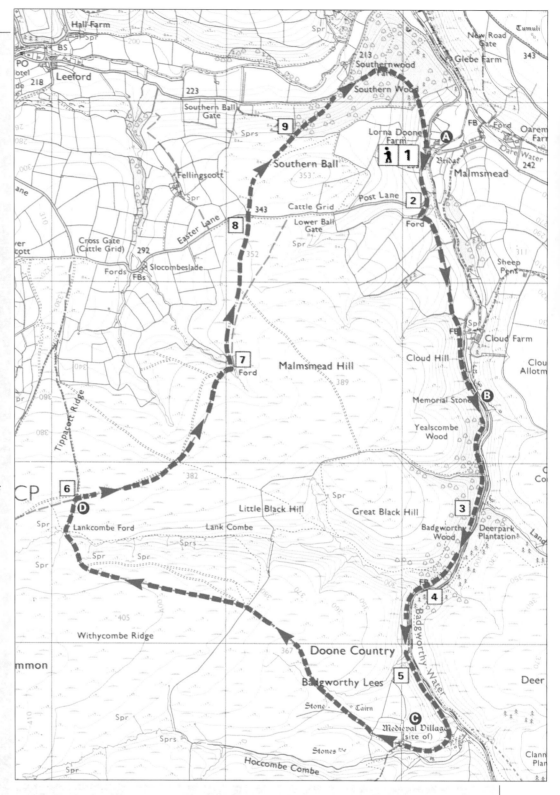

the ford then head for the signpost at the top of the hill. Note that this part of the path is very boggy — keeping slightly to the right of the main path misses the worst of the problem.

6 At the post at the top of Brendon Common **D** turn right to follow the

obvious track down to the second ford, ignoring all side paths and keeping to the signed route.

7 Where the track divides, keep to the left, heading straight to the road.

8 At the roadway, cross straight over, following the

signpost for the footpath to Malmsmead.

9 At the edge of the woodland, do not go through the field gate, but turn left to follow the path through the woods to a little lane that leads back to the car park where the walk began.

Carver Doone. The fictitious farm where the Ridds lived was given its location in the valley of Oare Water. Lorna Doone Farm stands at the confluence of the Oare and Badgworthy Waters, and Blackmore himself stayed nearby in a farm in the Oare Valley while writing the story.

Beyond the footbridge across the stream, the path becomes narrower

woodland on the opposite bank. This is an old sunken lane. The path makes its way down to the river by the footbridge to Cloud Farm, a Natural History Centre.

The path past the farm leads on to Oare, where R.D. Blackmore's grandfather was parson. This route, however, continues to follow the increasingly remote river valley, with the waters tumbling and gurgling over stones on the left and the heather-clad hillside of Exmoor to the right. The path now passes the memorial stone **B** to Richard Doddridge Blackmore, which was erected in 1969 to commemorate the publication of his celebrated romantic novel, *Lorna Doone*.

A DARK VALLEY

The walk now threads its way alongside the busy river through a woodland of old oak trees. A footbridge leads off towards the Oare Water valley, while Badgworthy Water flows in a series of small falls through the darkest part of the woodland. Valleys such as this are typical of the region. The underlying rock of Exmoor is very ancient, formed out of the mud and sand of the seabed when the whole area was covered by the ocean some 350 million years ago.

Over the ages the rivers have bitten ever deeper into the land, so that even a modest stream such as Badgworthy Water has cut a great cleft. The loamy, well-drained soil

allows plant life to flourish. The result is a typical, deep-wooded combe. Whether this is the actual combe selected by R.D. Blackmore for his story is uncertain: it is more likely that he drew on many such Exmoor clefts to create his secret, hidden valley.

SITES IN THE NOVEL

There are many other real locations that find their places in the novel, and one in particular is close to the walk. Oare Church, where the author's grandfather was rector from 1809 to 1842, was used as a setting for one of the key events of the story, the shooting of Lorna by

▲ *Badgworthy Water (above and below) forms the county boundary. The Ridds' farm may have been based on the Lorna Doone Farm (above left).*

Lank Combe where the rock formation known as the Water Slide is found.

and rougher and the view opens out to the seemingly featureless wastes of the Exmoor uplands. On leaving the woods, the path becomes a grassy track through the bracken and there is a much greater air of peace and secrecy about the valley. This is Hoccombe Combe. Today, only a few humps and scattered stones give any indication that this was the site of a medieval village ❻ and it is not too difficult to see this as a lost valley, home to a band of unscrupulous outlaws.

At this point the character of the route changes. It leaves the sheltered valley to climb up the hillside of tussocky grass and heather. This is typical Exmoor upland country. The soil of the plateau is thin and peaty, but just below the surface is a layer of impermeable clay. During periods of heavy rainfall the ground becomes waterlogged and this is the characteristic that has done so much to create the landscape. The water running off the moor swells the hill streams, giving them renewed force to dig even deeper channels.

It is a landscape in which the hills have been worn into smooth, gentle curves by the action of wind and rain; an undulating, featureless landscape of grassland and heather, stretching out to distant horizons. If it lacks the drama of the shattered tors of neighbouring Dartmoor, it nevertheless has its own character of genuine wildness.

MOORLAND VIEWS

The nature of the terrain varies very much with the weather. Fords are marked on the map which, in a dry summer, can become indistinguishable from the rest of the path, while in a wet season the whole upland area can become squelchy and boggy. But whatever the weather, the views from the high point of the moor ❼ are magnificent, spreading right across to the rocky coastline.

Once across the minor road down to Malmsmead, the path begins a steep and attractive descent down through woodland to lead back to the car park where the walk began.

Hoccombe Combe is supposed to be the hideout of the Doones.

Lorna Doone and Exmoor

The name 'Doone Country' is a tribute both to the imaginative power of the author, Richard Doddridge Blackmore, whose characters seem so vividly alive, and to the loving care with which he described this area of Exmoor in his novel, *Lorna Doone*. Yet the book could very easily have been a failure.

The book was first published in 1869 in three volumes, but sales were only modest. A junior partner in the publishers decided to risk reissuing it as a single volume and fortune favoured his move.

In 1871, Queen Victoria's daughter, Princess Louise, married the Marquis of Lorne. There were objections to the match, for although he was heir to the Duke of Argyll, he was not of royal blood. Public opinion, however, was all in favour of the love match and one journalist embellished the romance by connecting it to the fictitious Lorna Doone. The royal connection was enough to send the sales of the novel soaring.

The novel tells the story of two families, the virtuous Ridds and the villainous Doones. The latter are a band of outlaws hiding out in a remote and secret village on Exmoor, from which they emerge to raid and terrorise their neighbours. On one such raid they carry away a baby girl, who they raise as one of their own, Lorna Doone. Young John Ridd, the farmer's son, meets Lorna briefly as a boy and accidentally stumbles across the hidden Doone valley. Later, he returns as a man to rescue Lorna just as she is on the point of being forced into marriage with Carver Doone. The remainder of the book is taken up with the feud between the Ridds and the Doones. It is all highly charged romance, but it has a foundation in historical fact — the Doones themselves did exist — and the settings are based on actual places.

Lorna Doone being rescued from the evil Doones by her sweetheart John Ridd.

CASTLES AND COVES

A bracing walk to Dartmouth Castle and along the fortress cliffs of Little Dartmouth.

This walk presents the opportunity to see glorious sea views from a dramatic cliff-top path, to discover hidden coves and secret beaches and to visit the old Dartmouth Castle and Battery.

The walk begins at the National Trust car park at Little Dartmouth and proceeds along a high-sided lane that is typical of Devon. There are tantalizing glimpses of Start Bay to the right through gaps in the hedges and then a view of the Victorian Daymark **A**, a tower high up in the fields on the opposite headland, built to assist seafarers find the entrance to Dartmouth.

SEA DEFENCES

Further on, the walk passes behind old coastguard cottages and offers views of the entrance to the historic Dartmouth harbour and, on the opposite side of the river, of

MIKE WILLIAMS/NATIONAL TRUST PHOTOGRAPHIC LIBRARY. INSET: MARTIN SMITH/SWIFT PICTURE LIBRARY

BTA/ETB/SI

Kingswear Castle **B**, built in 1491 as part of a chain of sea defences.

The present Dartmouth Castle **C** was started in 1481 and was the most advanced fortification of its type at that time. Nearby is the church of St Petrox, dating from 1641-2.

From the castle, the route descends to Sugary Cove, before continuing along the coast to Blackstone Point. On the way you pass a coastguard lookout hut **D** with a flagpole and rack for notices. The grassy path now descends

▲ *On the rugged cliffs of south Devon, shag nests (inset) cling to the cliffside. Dartmouth Castle (left) commands an excellent strategic position at the harbour mouth.*

almost to sea level, and runs along the back of a shelf of rocks, which projects in jagged outcrops out into the sea. Further along a bridge crosses a narrow inlet where the waves rush in, thundering into the the cave **E** they have cut in the cliff.

Near here, at Compass Cove, one of the first submarine cables was laid across the Channel to Guernsey in 1860. A reminder of this is the telegraph marker pole **F**, showing where the cable lies.

From Compass Cove the walk climbs a steep, grassy hillside, continuing along the cliff top. When you reach Warren Point **G**, there are splendid views westwards along the whole length of Start Bay, as far as Start Point, with its lighthouse.

FACT FILE

⚹ On A379, Little Dartmouth, Devon

▱ Outdoor Leisure Map 20, grid reference SX 873491

miles 0 1 2 3 4 5 6 7 8 9 10 miles
kms 0 1 2 3 4 5 6 7 8 9 10 11 12 13 14 15 kms

◕ Allow 3 hours

▬ There are paths along the entire walk but the walk is not suitable in high winds or stormy weather as Blackstone Point is extremely exposed. The gullies at Blackstone Point are very slippery and must be avoided at all times

P National Trust car park at start point

T Infrequent bus service from Little Dartmouth to car park

🍴 Small café and toilets at Dartmouth Castle

THE WALK

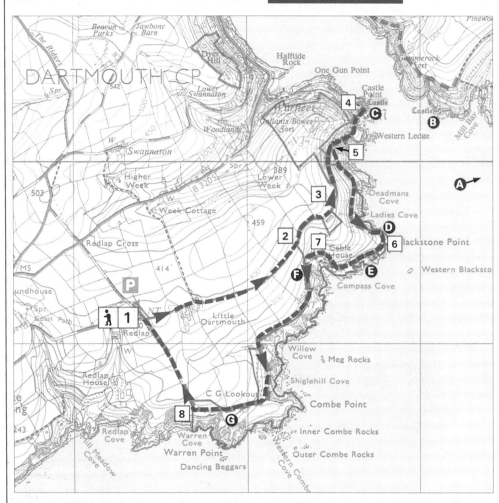

LITTLE DARTMOUTH – DARTMOUTH CASTLE

The walk starts at the National Trust car park at Little Dartmouth.

1 From car park follow bridleway signposted 'Dartmouth 2 miles'. Walk along metalled lane with views out to sea on right through gaps in hedges. Continue past entrance to Little Dartmouth House, between barns and through a metal farm gate. Walk on past white-painted cottages and two open barns. Go through another metal gate and continue on mud track with hedges on both sides. After a few hundred yards the Victorian Daymark **A** comes into view, high on opposite side of harbour entrance. Continue along track, passing a post with

diamond on top, to reach a stile next to a wooden gate.

2 Go over stile and, at marker post with blue and yellow arrows, follow direction of blue arrow, across the top of an open grassy hillside, which slopes down to the sea. At wooden gate follow blue arrow on post. Path becomes a metalled road behind coastguards' old cottages.

3 Go through wooden gate and continue along single track road. As road bears left and seaward hedge recedes there are good views of the entrance to the River Dart and you will see Kingswear Castle **B**. The road drops down through trees, past a stone cottage on left and sign 'Coast path Dartmouth 1 mile'. Continue straight on, past turning area,

and turn half-right through railings and down steps to Dartmouth Castle **C** and St Petrox Church.

4 After visiting the castle, return up steps to road, then fork left on to metalled path (ignoring yellow waymarked path), which runs parallel to road, past picnic area on left. Go down steps and carry along beside cliffs under trees. Continue on down to Sugary Cove and then follow steps and zig-zagging path back up hill through shady woodland with seats along the way. The path then levels out and at a junction of tracks take yellow waymarked path uphill to left.

5 Re-emerge on single track road opposite green-painted cottage. Fork almost immediately left, following

signpost 'Coastal path Little Dartmouth 1 3/4 miles'. Path is metalled at first and becomes a stony track beneath trees overlooking the sea. Go through gate and down the hill. At the flagstand with cross take the footpath off to right to visit a coastguard lookout hut **D**.

6 Rejoin main path, which continues downhill to Blackstone Point. Carry straight on, ignoring footpath to right. You are now close to the sea and this section of the walk could be wet on a windy day with spray from the sea. Continue, crossing a wooden bridge over a narrow inlet into caves **E**. Follow path along and up wooden bridge away from the sea. A short diversion here down into the next cove – Compass Cove – enables the walker to see the end of the original submarine cable laid underneath the Channel to Guernsey. Back at the top of the steps, go over the stile to climb the grassy slope.

7 At marker post follow a yellow waymarked path, turning left in front of seat. Continue on through wooden gate and past a telegraph cable marker **F**. Carry on, ignoring stile on right, to another stile. Cross, and continue along clifftop. Cross over a small wooden bridge, and follow path around curve of hill. At the wall, go through gap and continue along path to right alongside wall. You are now approaching Warren Point **G** and there are good views of Start Point.

8 The path turns right by a fence, which leads away from sea. Go through kissing gate and alongside hedge at edge of fields towards Little Dartmouth Farm (ahead to right), through gates and back to car park.

A DANGEROUS BEAUTY

17

DEVON

TIM WOODCOCK. INSET: PAUL STERRY/NATURE PHOTOGRAPHERS LTD

Along a steep-sided valley and through a fishing village

TIM WOODCOCK

The walk passes over moorland, with wide views along the Devon coast, and along the deep and beautiful wooded valley of the Lyn. It visits the popular resort of Lynmouth and a famous beauty spot, Waters Meet. The walk as

◀ *The joining of two streams at the aptly named Waters Meet makes a favourite spot for walkers. Watersmeet House, at the left, is a café.*

FACT FILE

- ✳ Lynmouth and the valley of the Lyn River, north-east Devon

- ⊡ Pathfinder 1214 (SS 64/74), grid reference SS 744488

- ◔ 2 hours

  miles 0 1 2 3 4 5 6 7 8 9 10 miles
  kms 0 1 2 3 4 5 6 7 8 9 10 11 12 13 14 15 kms

- ◣ Easy walking by the river, but there is a steep climb and descent along the sides of the valley

- P On the A39 at Waters Meet, or in Lynmouth

- ⊙ All facilities available in Lynmouth; there is a café at Waters Meet

- WC In Lynmouth and Waters Meet

▲ *The fishing village of Lynmouth can be glimpsed in this view from Oxen Tor. Wood vetch (inset), the Biblical tare and a member of the pea family, beautifies the paths and lanes of Devon.*

described begins at the car park above the café in Waters Meet, but it could equally well begin from Lynmouth ⓓ.

After a very short walk down the busy A39 Lynmouth road, walkers join a footpath that leads uphill through woodland. Once clear of the woods, the path emerges at the low earthen ramparts of an Iron Age enclosure, Myrtleberry North Camp

THE WALK

WATERS MEET – LYNMOUTH

The walk's starting point is the car park above the Watersmeet Café on the A39.

1 From the car park on the A39 at Waters Meet, walk downhill along the road for a few paces. Opposite the small car parking space, turn left off the road to take the footpath going steeply uphill through the woodland. Signposted to Lynmouth, it leads past the Iron Age enclosure **A**.

2 Where the path divides, continue straight on up the steps.

3 At the top of the hill continue following the path to the right, in the direction signposted to Lynton and Lynmouth. There is a sharp dip along the way **B**.

4 Where the path brings the first view of Lynmouth Harbour **C**, the way divides. Turn right, down towards the river valley, along the path indicated by a signpost reading 'Lynmouth ¾ mile'.

5 Where the broad track swings round to the right, continue straight on down the narrow path between high stone walls to Lynmouth **D**.

6 At the roadway, turn left, then right to cross over the bridge, then immediately right again, down the road signposted to the Waters Meet footpath. Continue following the riverside road **E**, passing Middleham Gardens, which can be seen on the opposite bank, until the road gives way to a footpath. Continue on this path, ignoring turnings off to the left.

7 After about 1½ miles (2.4 km), the clearly marked path crosses the footbridge and continues on the opposite bank. By the next footbridge, which is not crossed, is the site of the former Lynrock mineral water factory **F**.

8 At Waters Meet continue to follow the path uphill that leads straight ahead. Ignore the first path that turns sharply right, signposted A39, and take the next right (not the path that continues straight ahead at this point, marked 'Auntie's Path'). Return to the road and the car park.

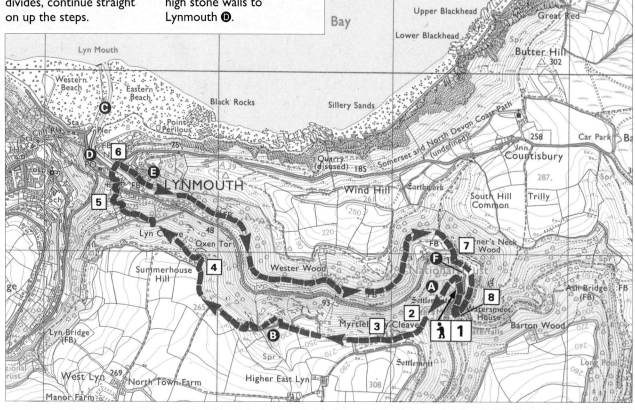

A. It continues uphill to the open moorland of bracken and heather, the way being clearly marked by steps cut into the hillside.

THE RIM OF THE VALLEY

As you climb steadily upwards fine views appear, looking back to the dark green cleft of the river valley and forward to Lynton, perched on the cliffs high above the sea. Once the rim of the valley is reached the path evens out to run on a ledge a little way above the tree-line. At times the view opens up so that you can look right down to the East Lyn river, a shining ribbon between the trees. Even at this height you can hear the roar of the river as it rushes down between the rocks.

The best viewpoint is from a stone seat, built beside the path in 1955. It is not a bad place to pause, because a small stream has dug a deep coomb, or valley, into the hillside **B**, and the path is about to zig-zag down through dense, dark woodland, mainly oak and birch, before winding its way up the other side. Here the rock thrusts its way

washed stone cottages, before the roadway and Lynmouth appear.

There has been a settlement here since before the Norman conquest, for this is one of the few sheltered spots on this notoriously dangerous coast. It continued for centuries as a small fishing village, but early in the 19th century it began to acquire a new role as a seaside resort.

A VICTORIAN RESORT

Among the early visitors was the poet Shelley, who eloped and brought his young bride here in 1812. Other Romantic poets came and were enthusiastic about the scenery, helping to ensure its popularity. There are still features of the Victorian resort to be seen. In 1890 Lynmouth was linked to Lynton, on the cliff tops above, by a cliff railway that still runs. One of the most

through the ground, presenting an interesting mixture of rock types owing to the fact that this valley represents a meeting between rounded sandstones and angular slates.

▲The Rhenish tower on the sea wall at Lynmouth is a replica of one built by a General Rawdon in 1860 to store salt water for baths at his home.

THE DOWNWARD PATH

The effort of climbing down into the little valley and up again is rewarded by some of the best views of the whole walk. Ahead one looks out to the coast, and the village and bay of Lynmouth; turning back you are able to see the whole extent of the Lyn Valley. The canopy of trees forms an almost complete cover, broken only by the river itself and

▼The waters of the East Lyn rush over tumbled rocks at a point just before the river enters Lynmouth.

▲The climb from Waters Meet is rewarded with the view over the tree-decked valley from Myrtleberry Cleave.

the roadway that accompanies it.

Shortly afterwards the descent begins; a steep, narrow path swinging round a rocky outcrop to make its way down through the woodland. As the path gets nearer to Lynmouth, it becomes more pronounced, bounded by mossy stone walls and bordered by impressive mature trees. Finally the path emerges between attractive white-

prominent landmarks by the harbour is the replica of the Rhenish tower built by a retired colonel and destroyed in the 1952 flood.

The walk leaves the town by the riverside, and its character changes from upland to river valley. A plaque near the start of the walk records the fact that the whole Waters Meet estate was given to the National Trust in 1936. The path stays close to the East Lyn, which rushes along between massive boulders, now cascading in small falls over the rocks, now spreading out

TIM WOODCOCK

into deep, clear pools. It is a famously picturesque river, but still retains something of the fierceness of the stream that burst into flood in 1952. There is a reminder of the disaster by one of the footbridges, where a stoneware bottle set in the rock is all that remains of the Lynrock mineral water factory ❻.

Beyond this point the valley sud-

◀ *A bottle set into the wall near Waters Meet marks the flooding of the Lynrock mineral water works in 1952.*

denly opens out. It is something of a surprise to come upon the house of Myrtleberry, with its ornate Victorian greenhouse, followed by Watersmeet House, now the café. This spot appealed to the Reverend W S Halliday, who in 1832 built Watersmeet House, inscribing a poem by Wordsworth above the door. It is not suprising that Waters Meet was much favoured by the Romantics, for here a waterfall rumbles below high crags, making a beautiful ending to the walk.

The Lynmouth Disaster

The River Lyn is composed of two branches, the East and West Lyn, which rise high on Exmoor and run down to the sea at Lynmouth, some 1,000 feet (300 metres) below the source. For most of the year, this is an attractive, fast-flowing river, bustling along as it threads its way over and through the boulders that litter its path. But heavy rainfall on Exmoor soon saturates the high moorland; trickles become streams, streams become rivers and the rivers join, to crash downhill and swell the waters of the East Lyn. This is what happened during the night of 15th August 1952.

Early August had been a period of heavy rainfall throughout south-west England. The ground was already waterlogged when thunderstorms brought torrential rain to the region. In places the rainfall may have been as much as 12 inches (30 cm), and it has been estimated that 3,000 million gallons (13,500 million litres) of water fell on the area that drains into the East and West Lyn rivers.

Flooding was inevitable, but disaster turned to outright tragedy because the worst of the damage came at night, long after families had retired to bed. The first cottages to be affected were a group right beside the river, in the Middleham area. Between 8 and 9 pm, the waters began to rise and nine of the 10 cottages were evacuated. The elderly inhabitants of the tenth house chose instead to wait on the upper floor. When the flood waters hit Lynmouth the cottages were simply swept away and today no trace of them remains. The area is now Middleham Gardens,

The morning after: police officers survey the devastation wrought in Lynmouth by the flooding of the West Lyn and East Lyn.

HULTON PICTURE LIBRARY

across the river from the footpath.

The floods, carrying a surge of debris on their churning waters, swept away the main road bridge and undermined the banks so that houses collapsed into the torrent. By daybreak the devastation was clear. Hundreds of people were homeless and 34 had lost their lives.

Lynmouth was totally rebuilt. Much of what now seems to be a charming old seaport is less than half

a century old. Most importantly, steps were taken to ensure that the disaster could never be repeated.

Near the mouth of the river, boulders were bulldozed away to ensure that the waters could escape into the sea. Bridges were built higher and wider to take the flow of water: the high-arched stone bridge near Waters Meet may look picturesque, but its design is wholly practical. The simple footbridges are lightly built of wood and designed to be swept clear away so that no debris could now impede the flow of water and cause flooding.

Away from the crowds in the heart of the Devon countryside

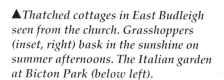

▲*Thatched cottages in East Budleigh seen from the church. Grasshoppers (inset, right) bask in the sunshine on summer afternoons. The Italian garden at Bicton Park (below left).*

East Budleigh Ⓐ, where this walk begins, lies in a quiet part of the Otter Valley, about 2 miles (3.2 km) north of Budleigh Salterton. It is an attractive village associated with Sir Walter Raleigh whose birthplace, Hayes Barton, can be seen from Hayes Lane, a little over 1 mile (1.6 km) west of the village.

The walk includes a stretch of the bank of the River Otter Ⓓ and an opportunity to visit Bicton Park Ⓒ, well known for its Italian garden, brilliant displays of shrubs and bedding plants, farm museum and narrow-gauge railway, complete with a steam locomotive, Woolwich.

ITALIAN GARDEN

A stream overhung with ferns and flowers — including red valerian and wild mignonette — runs through East Budleigh and is crossed by little bridges that lead to rows of colour-washed cob and thatched cottages.

The village church dates from the 12th century and has a collection of intricately carved bench ends. The pew where the Raleigh family worshipped can be found immediately in front of the pulpit. It is dated 1537, which makes it one of the

* East Budleigh, west of the A376, about 2 miles (3.2 km) north of Budleigh Salterton

Pathfinder 1330 (SY 08/18), grid reference SY 065848

miles 0 1 2 3 4 5 6 7 8 9 10 miles
kms 0 1 2 3 4 5 6 7 8 9 10 11 12 13 14 15 kms

Allow 2 hours

Mostly flat. Long grass might be encountered. Great care is needed at Stage 7 where the route crosses the A376

P Car park and information panel close to church in East Budleigh

Pubs and restaurants in East Budleigh. All facilities at Bicton Park, which is open every day March–October 10am–6pm, and 11am–4pm in October. Entrance fee. Tel. (01395) 568465

WC Close to church

THE WALK

EAST BUDLEIGH

*The walk begins at the car park south of the church in East Budleigh **A**. The car park is signposted off the corner of Hayes Lane where it joins East Budleigh's main street.*

1 From the car park, turn left and, with the car park on your left, walk up towards East Budleigh church. Pass the church on your left and turn right into Vicarage Road (signposted to Newton Poppleford). Walk along Vicarage Road for about 100 yards (90 metres).

2 Look carefully on the left of the road for a wooden gate and footpath sign (set back from the roadside). Turn left as indicated and follow the path straight on with the hedge on your left and a sports field on your right. The path bears right to cross a wooden stile. Now continue over another stile and keep straight on over the next wooden stile, which brings you to the minor road running west to Yettington and east to Otterton.

3 Turn left along the road for a short distance and look carefully for a stile and yellow arrow footpath sign crossing the hedge on your right. This is not marked on the map but leads immediately over the hedge to join the route on the corner at the top of

the field.

4 Follow the hedgerow down (on your right) into the dip for about 60 yards (54 metres) and look for a small wooden gate on your right, which could be partly concealed by undergrowth. Turn right through the gate, then immediately bear left along the edge of a field with the hedge on your left. Follow the path as the hedge beside you becomes a row of pollarded sycamores leading to a track. Follow the track in the direction of the main road, the A376.

5 Just before the main road, turn left following the sign for St Mary's Church down a walled path with woods on your left. Ahead of you are the arches of a ruined church. To the right of them is St Mary's Church. Beside the church is the Rolle mausoleum **B**. Beyond the church you will see some of the lawns and trees of Bicton Park **C**. Bear right, leaving the church on your left, and follow another walled path in the direction of the main road. Be very careful here as the path is concealed from traffic and the exit abuts the road directly.

6 At the main road, be extra watchful for traffic. Cross over and bear left to a footpath sign on your right.

7 Turn right and follow the path downhill. This

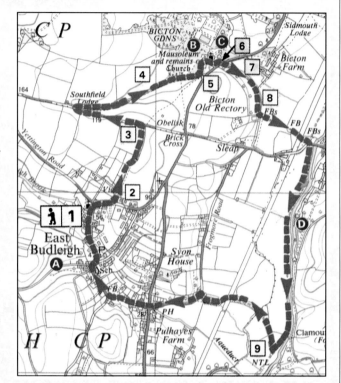

leads you along a path overshadowed by trees beside a small stream.

8 When you see a small wooden gate ahead, a little to your right, follow the path as it bears left over the stream. The path leads you over the disused railway and a grassed area to the bridge over the River Otter **D**. Turn right to cross the road just before the bridge and take the path running beside the river. Continue past a small bridge — Clamour Bridge — and walk along to a narrow water conduit. Do not cross this.

9 At this point there are

several paths. Do not take the obvious track on the right but turn sharp right along a raised path that you will see running over the water meadows, at first almost parallel with the river. This bears left over a stile. Follow the raised path round a small pumping station to join a track. Bear right towards East Budleigh. Turn left when you reach the minor road and follow the lane to the main road, the A376 opposite the Rolle Arms. Cross the road and continue in the direction of the village centre back to the car park.

earliest pews in England that is inscribed with a date.

Beside the church is the Rolle mausoleum **B**. It was designed by the 19th-century architect Augustus Pugin. The Rolle family built Bicton House (now the Devon School of Agriculture) in 1730.

The route skirts Bicton Park, formerly Bicton Gardens, which covers over 60 acres (24 hectares). It was laid out by Henry Rolle to designs by André le Nôtre, who designed the grounds of Versailles. Special features are the pinewood — one of the finest in Britain — and the Italian garden. The Countryside Museum houses a fine collection of farm equipment.

A later section of the walk follows the River Otter, which runs into Lyme Bay. Wild flowers grow in the water meadows and along the riverside — stands of yellow flag iris, rushes and purple loosestrife. Pink shaded cliffs, pitted with the tunnels of sand martins and draped in ivy and honeysuckle, overshadow the water. White-breasted dippers can be seen standing in the shallows.

THE LANDMARK TRUST. BOTTOM PIC: ANDREW CLEAVE/NATURE PHOTOGRAPHERS LTD

A channel crossing to the wildlife haven of Lundy Island

The BBC's national shipping forecast may have made Lundy a household name, but few will know anything else about this remarkable island. Viewed from Pembroke or from the North Devon coast, the island appears to float in the Bristol Channel like a huge whale. On closer inspection it is found to be a granite mass, 3 miles (4.8 km) long and ½ mile (800 metres) wide, which rises precipitously 400 feet (120 metres) from the surrounding and exceptionally clear sea. Topped by green fields, it now sports a small working community of some 17 inhabitants, is famous for its bird life and flora and holds many relics bearing testimony to its rich and colourful history.

NO TRAFFIC

The trip on the *MS Oldenburg* is an adventure in itself. Landing is like taking a pleasant step back in time. There are no cars on the island and

FACT FILE

* Lundy Island, off the North Devon Coast, Bristol Channel

* Pathfinder 1213 (SS 44/54 and part of SS 14), grid reference SS 146438

miles 0   1   2   3   4   5   6   7   8   9   10 miles
kms 0 1 2 3 4 5 6 7 8 9 10 11 12 13 14 15 kms

* Allow 3 hours

* Walk suitable all year. Crossing from mainland can be affected by weather

* **P** River Bank car park in Bideford. At the end of the pier in Ilfracombe

* **T** Day return trips with sailings from either Ilfracombe or Bideford. Average sailing time 2½ hours. Check with Lundy Office, Tel. (01237) 470422

* The Marisco Tavern sells its own beer brewed on the island and serves hot meals; open all day. Accommodation should be booked in advance by contacting the Landmark Trust, Tel. (01628) 825925

▲*Lundy is home to under 20 people, but the population swells to over 200 when the ferry delivers day-trippers. Thrift (below) grows easily on coasts, its long roots reaching deep into poor soil.*

the Landmark Trust (an architectural restoration charity that administers Lundy on behalf of the National Trust) has done a remarkable job in preserving a small working community whose granite

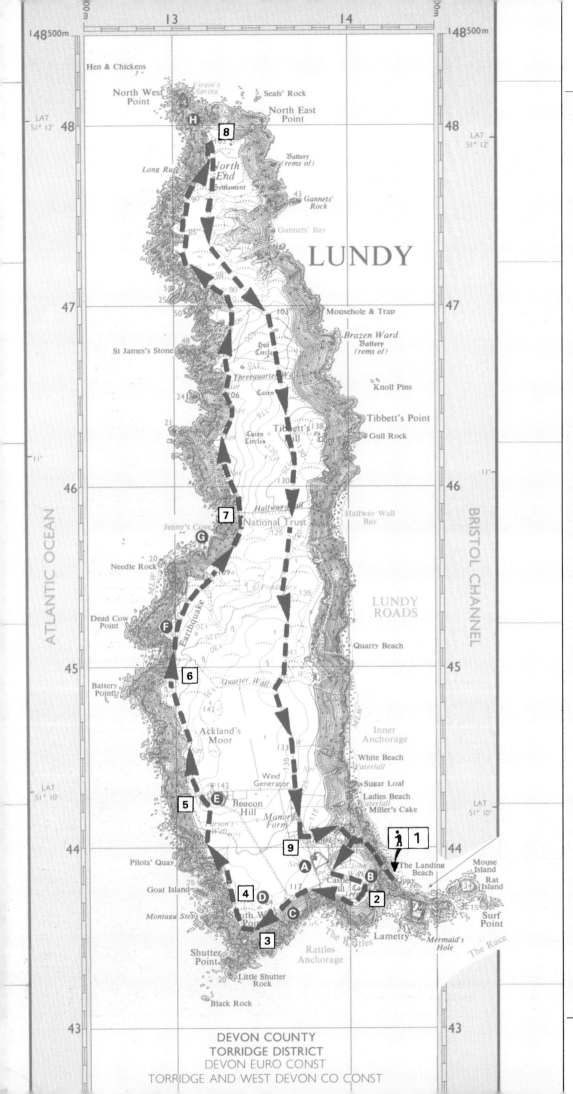

LUNDY

THE WALK

LUNDY ISLAND

The landing beach on Lundy Island is the starting point. Note that disembarkation from the ship MS Oldenburg is by a launch to the beach (there is no pier or harbour jetty) and this shuttle method can take some time. All passengers are given the same amount of time on the island.

1 Ascend the steeply rising beach road until it levels off, reaching the gently domed top of the island. St Helena's Church **Ⓐ** stands to the right and contains identification charts for flora and fauna. Turn left and continue along the road to the castle **Ⓑ**.

2 Bear right and cross the top of the cliffs to pass Benjamin's Chair **Ⓒ**. A little further on the right you pass Kistvaen burial chamber before reaching the Rocket Pole and Rocket Pole Pond **Ⓓ**.

3 Below here is the great chasm or Devil's Limekiln, but do not attempt to descend except in dry, windless conditions. This point overlooks the bay just north of Shutter Point, the scene of the shipwreck of *HMS Montagu*.

4 Follow the edge of south-west field in a northerly direction to pass through a gate into the cemetery **Ⓔ** behind the lighthouse compound (the Old Light).

5 Leave the cemetery and take the gate below the lighthouse. Continue to follow the Westside Path until, some 100 yards (90 metres) before the Quarter Wall is reached, a grassy bank slopes down to the left. From this a path descends to the Battery overlooking the sea.

▶ **6** Re-ascend to the Western Path and continue north bearing left where the path forks to observe the rift of the Earthquake **F**. Continue along the coast to observe fine views of Jenny's Cove **G**. The path now leads inland up the Punchball Valley. At the head of the valley bear left to find the Cheeses and the Halfway Wall.

▶ **7** Continue northwards along the Western Path crossing the Threequarter Wall, then pass the Devil's Slide on the cliffs below to reach the North Light **H** at the end of the island.

▶ **8** Return south on the central track that leads directly into the village.

▶ **9** Turn left in front of the Marisco Tavern and follow the path across the fields, descending to the trees surrounding Millcombe House. The path leads down steps behind the house, first to join its front drive and then the beach road leading back to the sea and the *MS Oldenburg*.

▲ *Lundy's Victorian church, St Helena's, is by the village and is large enough to hold the parishioners several times over.*

buildings comprise a small village, church and farm. There are fine views east to the North Devon coast, some 11 miles (18 km) distant while, to the west, 4,000 miles (6,400 km) of ocean separate Lundy from land. Space, peace and tranquillity pervade the place. All of these elements, combined with the outstanding natural history of the island, make for a fascinating walk.

Leaving the disembarkation point, the stony track passes a cave and battered cannon. The cannon is thought to have been thrown down from above by a party of French privateers during the reign of William III. Further up on either side can be seen a species of plant endemic to the island — the Lundy cabbage. This has long straggly stalks which bear small yellow flowers from mid-June to mid-August.

THE KINGDOM OF HEAVEN

Visitors are welcome to enter St Helena's Church **A**, but are requested to close the door behind them to keep out the sheep. The church was built in 1896 by the Rev Hudson Heaven who then owned the island and it became known as 'the Kingdom of Heaven'.

A PIRATE BASE

The castle **B** dates from 1244 and was built by Henry III in an attempt to control the island following a century of rule by the notorious de Marisco family. During the reign of King John (1167-1216), William de Marisco used the island as a base for his piratical activities.

Further along the route is a view of Benjamin's Chair **C**, a grassy platform named after a ship that was wrecked in the bay below. Shortly after this you may spot a mound, the remains of an ancient burial chamber called Kistvaen, rising from the bracken and gorse. Rocket Pole Pond **D** appears beyond Rocket Pole, where practice rockets carrying life-lines used to be fired. A few breadcrumbs thrown into the pond result in frenzied feeding by the mirror carp lurking within its depths.

In summer, large patches of basil and thyme may be seen around here. Look also for yarrow, with its white flowers and fern-like leaves.

GRANITE FEATURES

The next feature on the walk is the great rift hole of the Devil's Limekiln, the steep granite walls of which plunge 300 feet (90 metres). Following this is a fine view of the western coast and a bay where Lundy's most famous wreck occurred, that of the battleship *HMS Montagu* which foundered here in May 1906 during thick fog.

The cemetery **E** reveals some of the island's past and was the site of the original St Elan's Chapel; the foundations can still be seen close to the wall of the lighthouse compound. Four ancient memorial stones inscribed in Latin now stand against the west wall, attributable to the Christian community that survived here after the collapse of Roman rule in Britain.

THE LIGHTHOUSE

The Old Light was completed in 1819 by Trinity House. At a height of 567 feet (173 metres) above sea level, it was the highest in Britain – alas too high, for it was often in cloud when all was clear at sea level, hence the construction of Lundy's other two working lighthouses (the North and South Lights). The Battery is positioned further along beneath the Westside Path. It was built as a signal station in 1863 and is reached by descending a steep path marked by a small stone cairn. At the base of the path

▶ *Lundy's position made it a natural fortress in the past and a pirates' lair. The Battery ruins are on the west coast.*

The Growling Bird

Lundy has long been associated with the puffin. In 1939 some 3,500 pairs nested on the island, but sadly the population now only numbers some 100 pairs. These figures are reflected throughout Britain and are thought to be because of the decline in the sandeel, one of its main sources of food. From May to July puffins can be seen nesting along the cliffs of Battery Point, Jenny's Cove and the north end of the island.

Although often called a sea parrot, the puffin is actually an auk – a dumpy-bodied, relatively large-headed bird belonging to the *Alcidae* family. Its large head, curious eye markings and colourful, triangular-shaped beak, banded red, orange and bluish grey, give it a clown-like appearance.

The puffin visits land between May and August to lay and incubate its one egg; the rest of the year it remains far out to sea. It nests in a burrow dug in the turfy tops of sea cliffs, although it may use a deserted rabbit hole. The puffin's call, which resembles a deep growl, can often be heard emanating from its burrow when nothing else is visible. Its food, for which it dives and swims underwater with great skill and speed, consists of sardines and sandeels. It often flies back to its nest with as many as 10 fish neatly arranged in a row along its bill. Visitors to Lundy Island are asked not to disturb the birds.

Although much depleted, there is still a puffin colony on Lundy. This appealing-looking bird appears on the island's stamps.

After paying £9,870 for Lundy Island in 1834, William Heaven built Millcombe House there as a family seat.

(thrift) are quite outstanding during May and June. The Threequarter Wall is followed by a splendid view of the impressive 400-foot (122-metre) granite slab of Devil's Slide. Wild goats inhabit these cliffs, while dolphins and grey seals frequent the waters below. The North Light ❶ marks the northern end of the walk.

AN ISLAND HERD

On the east coast, sika deer, introduced in the 1920s, live in the dense rhododendron thickets, generally appearing only at dawn or dusk. The brown Soay sheep are more prominent, as are the Lundy ponies — now an officially recognized herd. These are a handsome dun colour and originally a cross between New Forest and Welsh Mountain ponies. Lundy is on the western migratory route for birds and in spring and autumn unusual species may be spotted. In spring many warblers arrive, while in autumn breeding birds from North America such as the blackpoll warbler and American robin have also been recorded.

On the track to the main street of the village are cottages and farm buildings, and the working brewery. In front of the Marisco Tavern lies a long granite stone said to have been the lid of a grave that contained giant human bones. Two enormous skeletons were unearthed in 1850, one of a man estimated at 8 ½ feet (2.5 metres) and the other of a woman of 7 ¾ feet (2.3 metres). The age of the bones was never established and they were reburied in the cemetery near the Old Lighthouse.

are two roofless granite houses where the gun crew lived. Below this, granite steps descend through a rock cutting to the firing platform where two George III cannons and the domed shell of the gunhouse still remain. When the weather was foggy a blank round was fired every 10 minutes.

THE EARTHQUAKE

The finest coastal scenery and birdlife on the island lies along the Westside Path. Here is the curious rift some 80 feet (24 metres) deep known as the Earthquake ❻. This feature was reputedly created by tremors from the Lisbon earthquake of 1755. Three types of heath constitute much of the wild foliage at this point: common heather, or ling, with small pink flowers; bell heather, with purple flowers; and cross-leaved heath with bell-like pink

North of the Threequarter Wall, the Devil's Slide of sheer granite drops dramatically down the cliffside.

flowers. Punchball Valley follows and is so-named because of the hollowed-out, saucer-shaped stone found near the bed of the stream.

Jenny's Cove ❻ marks one of the best areas to view the sea-birds that breed here. From March to August look out for puffins, razorbills and guillemots. Kittiwakes, fulmars and many other types of gull are seen all year round.

Just before the Halfway Wall is a pinnacle-like formation of granite called the Cheeses. From this point it is the natural history of the coast and cliffs that becomes the major attraction. The carpets of sea pinks

FAIR WIDECOMBE

DEVON

Through high moorland scenery to a remarkable prehistoric site

Widecombe, where the walk begins, has been made famous by the song *Widecombe Fair* and its account of the doings of Old Uncle Tom Cobley and all. The fair is still held on the second Tuesday in September. The place would certainly be a popular tourist spot even without the well-known song, for it typifies the charm of the Dartmoor village. Sitting in a hollow surrounded by moorland, Widecombe's

FACT FILE

✴ Widecombe in the Moor, 10 miles (16km) north-west of Newton Abbot

🗺 Outdoor Leisure Map 28, grid reference SX 718767

miles 0 1 2 3 4 5 6 7 8 9 10 miles
kms 0 1 2 3 4 5 6 7 8 9 10 11 12 13 14 15 kms

◔ Allow 4 hours

⬛ One long ascent and descent, and sections over open moorland. Walking boots and weatherproof clothing are essential

P Car parks at Widecombe

🍴 The pub in Widecombe in the Moor serves food

CHRIS CHAPMAN, INSET: MIKE READ/SWIFT PICTURE LIBRARY

village green, with an inn and an old smithy, is overlooked by the tall granite tower of the parish church of St Pancras **A**.

There is the same monumental solidity inside the church, typified by the monolithic pillars of the nave, but its chief glory lies in its ornate roof bosses. Some are carved with complex geometric patterns, others show plants and animals. Three one-eared rabbits chase each other round

CHRIS CHAPMAN

◀ *On the moorland of Hamel Down is a Bronze Age site called Two Barrows, though only one mound survives.*

▲ *The impressive, granite-built Church of St Pancras in Widecombe in the Moor dates mostly from the 14th century. The meadow pipit (inset) thrives on the open moorland.*

a ring, while a tethered scapegoat looks suitably miserable. An angel looks across, perhaps with an air of disapproval, at a green man, an ancient fertility symbol.

The walk begins by following a quiet country road, with a clear little stream gurgling alongside, but soon turns off along a surfaced road to climb Hamel Down. The road is

THE WALK

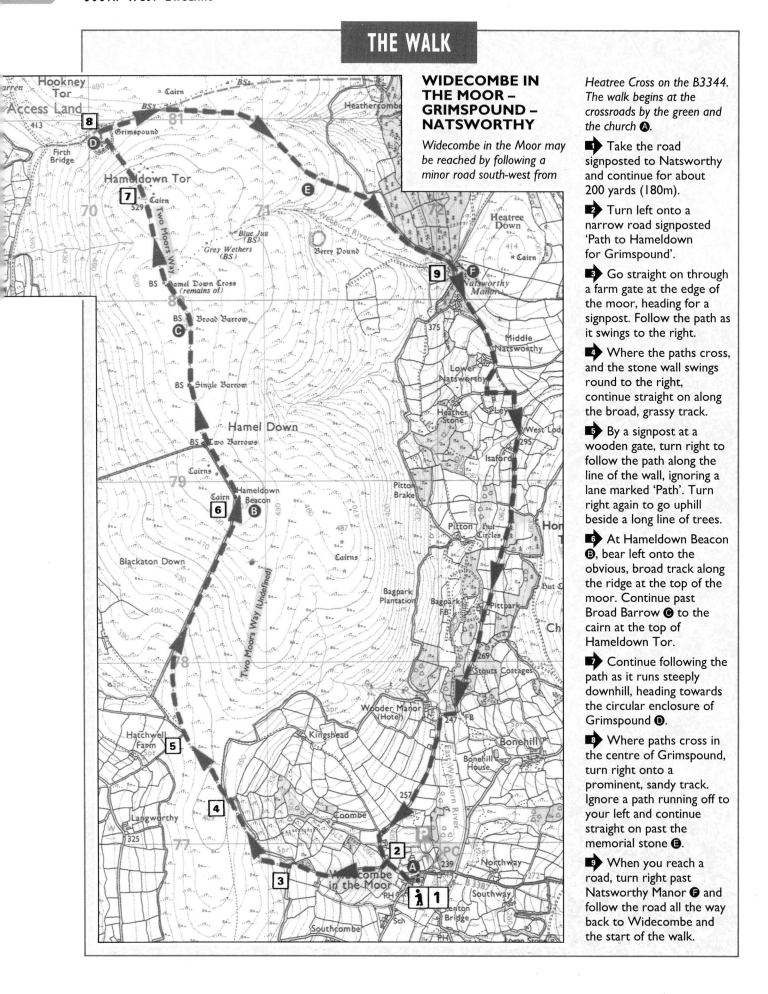

WIDECOMBE IN THE MOOR – GRIMSPOUND – NATSWORTHY

Widecombe in the Moor may be reached by following a minor road south-west from Heatree Cross on the B3344. The walk begins at the crossroads by the green and the church Ⓐ.

1 Take the road signposted to Natsworthy and continue for about 200 yards (180m).

2 Turn left onto a narrow road signposted 'Path to Hameldown for Grimspound'.

3 Go straight on through a farm gate at the edge of the moor, heading for a signpost. Follow the path as it swings to the right.

4 Where the paths cross, and the stone wall swings round to the right, continue straight on along the broad, grassy track.

5 By a signpost at a wooden gate, turn right to follow the path along the line of the wall, ignoring a lane marked 'Path'. Turn right again to go uphill beside a long line of trees.

6 At Hameldown Beacon Ⓑ, bear left onto the obvious, broad track along the ridge at the top of the moor. Continue past Broad Barrow Ⓒ to the cairn at the top of Hameldown Tor.

7 Continue following the path as it runs steeply downhill, heading towards the circular enclosure of Grimspound Ⓓ.

8 Where paths cross in the centre of Grimspound, turn right onto a prominent, sandy track. Ignore a path running off to your left and continue straight on past the memorial stone Ⓔ.

9 When you reach a road, turn right past Natsworthy Manor Ⓕ and follow the road all the way back to Widecombe and the start of the walk.

◄Broad Barrow, on the summit of Hamel Down, is the most impressive of the burial sites. At the far extreme of the walk is Grimspound (right) where, 3,000 years ago, Bronze Age settlers kept their cattle in the winter.

bordered by stone walls roughly fashioned from granite boulders. Growing on top of the walls are old, gnarled trees, with their roots spread out around the stones.

As you climb, a fine view opens out behind you; Widecombe and its tower, surrounded by a patchwork of small fields, and the rough moorland and hill tops beyond, bristling with shattered rocks.

SLABS OF ROCK

The stone walls bordering the lane give way to high, grassy banks, and bracken begins to invade. The road becomes a rough track, and its cover of sandy earth grows thinner, eventually revealing impressive flat slabs of rock underfoot. Over the centuries, stones of this sort have been used to build everything from humble barns to grand houses.

The path ends at a farm gate, where the moorland proper begins. The route leads through a grassy hollow in an area of short-cropped turf, colourfully dotted with heather and gorse and grazed by ponies and

sheep. A few stunted trees and bushes have survived on these wind-swept uplands. A wall made up of massive blocks, some as much as 6 feet (1.8m) long, as well as smaller, more rounded stones, marks the farm boundary. Across a deep combe to your right, Kingshead Farm sits in a lonely spot high up on the moor. The path crosses a little ridge and drops down to the stone walls that mark the upper limits of the farms of the next valley.

The path changes direction again for the final ascent to the top of Hamel Down. This is a lovely section of moorland, richly coloured with gorse and heather. A line of beech trees, their branches bent by the prevailing winds, reach over to form a canopy for the little stream that rushes downhill, beside the path, over a series of small falls.

As you ascend, the stream narrows until it becomes no more than a succession of trickles draining off the moor, and rocks begin to poke through the thin surface soil. Great lumps of granite, sparkling with

mica and coloured by felspar, are mixed in with occasional chunks of crystalline quartz. This is a very lonely patch of moorland, with sheep, ponies and the occasional hovering kestrel your only company.

Where the trees come to an end, they are replaced by a stone wall of truly massive boulders and slabs. Whinchats, summer visitors here, are especially fond of the wall-top perches. At the sight of a walker, they fly on uphill, displaying their white-patched tails, until eventually they decide they have reached a safe distance, and find a new perch.

HIGH BEACON

At the top of Hameldown Beacon ❸ is a cairn and a stone dated 1854. From here, there is a magnificent panoramic view. To the west is the rolling moorland of central Dartmoor. Eastwards is a high ridge whose outline is marked with the broken slopes of the tors; beyond it are the more massive rocks of Haytor. The sea is visible to the south, beyond a line of hills, and to the north are the gentler hills and the lush, green farmland of central Devon, brightened in patches by the rich, red earth of ploughed fields.

The walk follows the ridge along the top of Hamel Down. Where the wall swings away to the left is the first of a series of prehistoric burial mounds. Two Barrows — though only one is now obvious — is a typical round barrow, a massive circular

◄Heading east from Grimspound, you pass a stone memorial to the crew of an RAF bomber that crashed on the moor.

Grimspound

The atmospheric remains of the Bronze Age settlement known as Grimspound provide a fascinating glimpse into the lives of the people who buried their dead in the great round barrows on the top of Hamel Down. Though today this is a lonely and inhospitable place, difficult to farm, some 3,000 years ago its prospects were different. The slopes were relatively easy to clear for pasture, and the thin soil suited the crude tools of the day.

Grimspound's well preserved hut circles have provided archaeologists with much information about the Bronze Age.

The people who lived here probably grew a few crops, but the bulk of their diet consisted of meat. They grazed cattle on the slopes in the summer, and kept them in a compound in the winter. The compound was surrounded by a substantial stone wall. Even the remains of this are impressive; in places, they are 3 feet (1m) high and 10 feet (3m) thick. The entrance can still be made out, with tall stones flanking a pavement of stone slabs.

Within the compound were around 20 circular houses with low stone walls. These would have been topped by conical roofs constructed of thatch, possibly bracken and heather, each supported by a central pole. The walls, complete with entrance passages curved to provide some shelter from the wind and rain, are still in evidence.

Some of the houses have survived better than others, but inside the best of them you can see the central stones that supported the roof pole. Domestic details such as cooking holes and stone shelves, which would probably have supported primitive bedding arrangements, are also clearly visible.

perfect, box-like straight lines. The hills on either side also display great contrast. To the right is the gentle rise of Hamel Down; to the left, the more jagged outlines of Honeybag Tor and Chinkwell Tor, where the rocks have erupted through the crests of the ridge.

You go steadily downhill and, as you do so, the character of the country begins to change. The fields are altogether lusher and greener, and the farms more closely packed together. Occasionally, the regularity is broken by patches of rough grass and by massive boulders too troublesome for the farmers to clear.

The road runs in and out of areas of woodland. Their green depths are a wilderness of tall ferns and mossy boulders. Beech and birch trees lean their branches over the road to create a green tunnel, and between the trees there are glimpses of farmhouses set comfortably against the slopes of the hill.

The road crosses a brown, peaty stream that tumbles down from the moorland, and you leave the woodland. Almost hidden behind a plantation of conifers and ornamental trees is the elegant, white-washed Wooder Manor, now a hotel. Finally, the tall tower of Widecombe church appears ahead, and you return to the village green.

mound with traces of a ditch outside, characteristic of the Bronze Age. Beyond it is a more decayed, single barrow, but by far the most impressive can be seen on the horizon, the aptly named Broad Barrow **C**. At 1,745 feet (532m), this is the high point of the walk. Beyond it, a cairn marks the end of the ridge, and the path heads steeply downhill. Soon the great circular enclosure of Grimspound **D** comes into view below you (see box).

The path away from Grimspound is a broad, sandy track across an otherwise empty expanse of heather moorland. Ponies, which seem quite unconcerned by the presence of walkers, are your only company here. To the right of the track stands a tall stone **E**, which bears a carved inscription on one side, and on the other a plaque explaining that it was here, on the 22 March 1941, that an RAF bomber crashed when returning from France, killing the crew.

The path leaves the moor at this point, going steeply downhill and past the edge of a conifer plantation to join the quiet country lane that runs back to Widecombe.

Initially, the lane runs between stone walls topped by slender birch trees. Having entered an area of woodland, it passes a grand house, Natsworthy Manor **F**, whose walls are hung with slate. Just beyond Natsworthy, the road bends past a delightful thatched cottage.

BEECH HEDGES

The intimacy of the lane, with trees rearing up from the walls, is in stark contrast to the open footpaths of the moor. At times, the banks reach well above head height. They are topped in places by stone walls, and elsewhere by beech hedges cut into

▶ *The country lane back from Natsworthy leads through an avenue of beech trees growing out of stone walls.*

BOTH PHOTOS: CHRIS CHAPMAN

CHRIS CHAPMAN INSET: M. GARWOOD/NHPA

A stroll around one of the loveliest villages in the West Country

▲Dating from the 17th century, the cottages of Broadhembury are undeniably picturesque. The speckled wood butterfly (right) flies locally in woodland clearings and on shady lanes.

Broadhembury lies in a deep combe, sheltered to the north and east by a steep wooded ridge. This walk climbs along sunken lanes and green paths, bright with flowers, to the crest of the combe, and follows the hillside, with spectacular views of this quiet area of Devon countryside. Deer can sometimes be seen in the deeper woodland, while buzzards soar over the open fields.

DELIGHTFUL COTTAGES

You step back almost 400 years as you enter Broadhembury **Ⓐ**. All the rows of cottages and houses, clustered around the square and tucked up narrow lanes, date from the early 17th century. They are built low beneath deep eaves of mossy thatch, and their rough-cast walls are colour-washed a soft cream.

Gardens spill over into a roadway, and mingle with the wild flowers on the verges and beside the River Tale, the little stream that flows down from the top of the combe.

The walk begins at St Andrew's Church, which dates mainly from the 14th and 15th centuries. It has a fine tower, and a beautiful vaulted porch with a tiny statue of St Andrew over the doorway. The Reverend Augustus Toplady, the composer of the hymn *Rock of Ages*, was vicar here from 1768 to 1778.

The local inn, the Drewe Arms, is named after Edward Drewe, Sergeant-at-Law to Elizabeth I. He became Lord of the Manor here in 1603, and built The Grange, the large 17th-century house that the route passes on the way into the village via Colliton Cross.

THE WALK

BROADHEMBURY – BARLEYCOMBE FARM

The walk begins by the church **Ⓐ** *at the centre of Broadhembury. To reach the village, turn off the A373 at Colliton Cross.*

1 Walk down to the square. Keep straight on, down to a little stone bridge over the River Tale. Cross it and turn right. Follow the lane as it bears left and begins a gentle upward climb past Marlpit Copse **Ⓑ**.

2 At a crossing track, turn left. Go steeply uphill through a wood to the top of the hill. Cross the stile in front of you and walk straight on past the gliding club **Ⓒ** on your left.

3 Bear right across a cattle grid, and follow a narrow metalled lane bordered by beech trees to a road. Turn right, and follow the road for about 200 yards (180m).

4 Turn right through a gate to follow a signposted bridleway back to the crest of the combe **Ⓓ**, where there is a magnificent view. Do not go through the metal gate, but bear left through a wooden gate and follow the path along the crest towards woodland, with the hillside dropping away to your right.

5 When the fence on your right ends, and Hanger Farm is below to your right, go straight on towards a gate. Go through it, and continue with the fence and woods close on your right. After about 100 yards (90m), the obvious track bears uphill away from the woods towards a gate. Ignore this, and keep straight on along the grassy path by the fence and trees to a wooden gate. Beyond it, follow the path along the edge of the woods.

6 When you reach a road, turn right and follow it all the way back to Broadhembury and the start of the walk.

---

edges. It leads through small copses where bluebells, wood anemones and wood sorrel grow and tiny streams run through deep channels overhung with ferns.

GLIDING ALONG

Near the top of the hill is a gliding club **Ⓒ**. You can quite often hear the howl of the wind on the launch cable as a glider climbs steeply into the sky, or see the gliders circling to gain height in the currents of rising air at the top of the combe.

A walk along the top of the combe leads you to a breathtaking viewpoint **Ⓓ**. Spread at your feet is the typical Devon countryside of rolling green hillsides and woods. Beyond, some 20 miles (32km) to the south-west, are the Haldon Hills, while Dartmoor broods in the west. A little to the south, the ground dips then rises to Hembury Hill Fort. Originally a Neolithic causewayed camp of around 2500BC, this was fortified in the Iron Age to enclose about 8 acres (3.2ha).

The return route first follows a woodland path, so thickly carpeted with bluebells in spring that you have no choice but to walk on them, then descends another sunken, flower-fringed lane into the village.

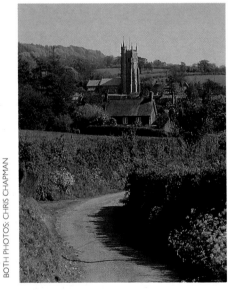

BOTH PHOTOS: CHRIS CHAPMAN

The route leaves the village by Long-go Lane, which passes Marlpit Copse **Ⓑ**, a reminder of an old way of improving soil. Marl (limy clay) was dug out and spread over the land by gangs of itinerant 'marlers'.

Beyond the copse, the lane becomes grassy and more deeply sunken, with wild flowers growing through tangled tree roots along the

◀The route from the village is along a typically deep, hedged Devon lane that offers a good view of the church. Further along, Long-go Lane (right) passes through fields between banks of yellow broom.

DEVON

The entrance to the church is through a lychgate with an unusual 'pattern' style, hinged to bring it up rather like a modern level crossing barrier. The church itself is remarkably handsome. It is basically 15th-century, built in the Perpendicular style. As so often in Devon, its most striking feature is the beautifully carved rood screen, with its elaborate patterns of vaulting — though it is also worth peering behind the organ to see a magnificent Baroque monument.

OVER THE BRIDGE

You follow a stream from the village to the bottom of a valley. The road crosses the Little Dart River at Stone Mill Bridge **B**. The stone mill still retains the remains of its overshot water-wheel. The water is brought to the mill along a wooden trough, or launder, and then falls into 'buckets' set on the rim of the wheel.

The route now turns to follow the Little Dart. This is nothing to do with the Dart that reaches the sea in South Devon; it is a tributary of the River Taw. At first, the valley is quite wide, with the road against the northern edge and the river meandering away to the south. The road runs between grassy banks that are

▲ *The route runs for over a mile (1.6km) along the Little Dart River, which is crossed by three bridges. Near the first bridge is an old watermill (below right). The field vole (left) can be found in areas with long grass.*

Along a wooded valley and across the grassy hills of Devon

The farmland lying between Dartmoor and Exmoor is one of the least-known parts of Devon. This walk explores some typical scenery. It begins in Chawleigh, a hilltop village whose houses are built of rough-hewn sandstone, sometimes disguised by paintwork and rendering. Near the start is an attractive thatched house, finished with thatch birds on the ridge. A short diversion takes you past the old stone primary school, with its hexagonal-paned cast-iron windows, to the village church **A**.

FACT FILE

- Chawleigh, 18 miles (28.8km) north-west of Exeter, off the A377

- Pathfinder 1275 (SS 61/71), grid reference SS 712124

  miles 0 1 2 3 4 5 6 7 8 9 10 miles
  kms 0 1 2 3 4 5 6 7 8 9 10 11 12 13 14 15 kms

- Allow 2½ hours

- Mostly minor roads and paths, with a few fairly steep ascents and descents. Muddy in places, and very muddy in wet weather. Walking boots are essential

- P Off road near the start

- The Chilcott Arms in Chawleigh

MIKE WILLIAMS. INSET: STEPHEN DALTON/NHPA

MIKE WILLIAMS

THE WALK

CHAWLEIGH – WEST BURRIDGE CROSS

The walk begins by the Chilcott Arms in Chawleigh.

1 Take the road down past the inn, signposted to Cheldon and Gidley Arms. Turn left to visit the church **A**, then return and go left to continue on the original road. Beyond Stone Mill Bridge **B** is a T-junction. Turn right. Where the road divides, bear right, signposted to Lapford.

2 The road bridges a small stream; immediately beyond that, turn left through a wooden gate to join the path beside the stream, keeping the stream on your right. The route follows the Little Dart River for 1 mile (1.6km), until the path rises up a grassy hill. Continue along the brow of the hill to a gate onto the roadway.

3 Go through and turn right. Follow the road uphill. It runs clear of the trees and a farm track appears on your left.

4 Turn right through the gate opposite the end of the track. Follow the path, keeping the bank with its crown of trees on your left-hand side. Follow the sunken lane ahead down through the woods. Where the path divides, continue straight on, crossing both the small streams, to East Leigh Farm.

5 Take the farm track between the house and the barn. Where the farm track divides, continue straight on and across the fields as indicated by the public footpath sign at the gate. Cross the high ground **C**, and head slightly to the left of the group of buildings ahead. The route goes round the left of a small enclosure ringed by trees to a road.

6 Cross over and take the path opposite, past a new house. At the end of the green lane, continue in the direction indicated by the waymark. About 50 yards (45m) left of where telegraph lines cross the rim of the valley, take the path downhill indicated by the waymark. Cross a stream and head half-right, keeping the hedgeline to your left. Join a grassy lane, which leads to the road. Turn left to return to the start of the walk.

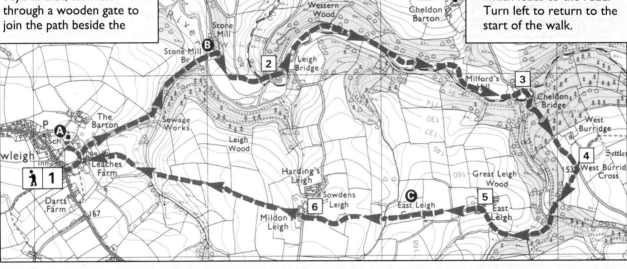

▼ *The green lane near the end of the walk offers this view of Chawleigh, dominated by its church tower.*

MIKE WILLIAMS

especially attractive in spring, when they are covered with primroses.

As the road enters the wooded part of the valley, the route turns off to follow a footpath alongside the river. At first it is a broad, grassy track between a lively river and a mixed woodland that clings to a steep, rocky hillside. Where the valley narrows, the path enters the woods, which by now reach down to the banks of the stream. Deer can often be glimpsed grazing in the woods, and herons stand statue-still beside the water.

There is a final, gentle climb up a grassy hill before you leave the path for another quiet country lane. The road goes steeply downhill to bridge a little rocky river gorge, then climbs just as steeply up the opposite side of the valley.

The return half of the walk is on footpaths. It begins by diving downhill along a sunken lane through the woods to a deep valley carved by several small streams. Then it climbs to a high plateau **C**, passing East Leigh Farm and some ruined farm cottages. Here, there are long views over a wide tract of countryside.

DOWN THE DIP

A final green lane offers an encouraging view of Chawleigh's church up ahead, but before it can be reached there is another downhill plunge between gorse bushes and one last climb to bring the footpath back to Chawleigh.

SLAPTON LEY

Leafy lanes and a coastal path round an important nature reserve

The South Hams district of Devon is a rich rural region of red earth with cob and thatch cottages. The market towns of Kingsbridge and Totnes are the only settlements of any size, but there are many small villages and prosperous farms tucked in among the rounded hills and patches of old woodland.

There are some wild and windswept headlands, but south of Torbay is a more gentle coastline of low cliffs and wide, sheltered bays. This walk combines a section of this coast with a ramble through the agricultural hinterland.

The starting point is outside the

FACT FILE

☀ Stokenham, 4½ miles (7.2km) east of Kingsbridge, on the A379

os Outdoor Leisure Map 20, grid reference SX 808428

miles 0 1 2 3 4 5 6 7 8 9 10 miles
kms 0 1 2 3 4 5 6 7 8 9 10 11 12 13 14 15 kms

◷ Allow 4 hours

⬢ Varied terrain: woodlands, fields, shingle, muddy banks, rocky clifftop paths and tarmac. Four fairly strenuous climbs. Walking boots are essential

P Car park near Stokenham's parish church

T For details of bus services, Tel. (01752) 664011

🏚 The Church House Inn and The Tradesman's Arms pub in Stokenham; the Village Inn and the Start Bay Inn in Torcross

🍴 Restaurants and tea-rooms in Torcross

wc In Torcross, and on Sands near Slapton Bridge (seasonal)

▲ *The shingle ridge of Slapton Sands curves around between the sea and the freshwater of Slapton Ley. The water rail (left) is wary, but may be glimpsed at the water's edge on the nature reserve. Beyond Widdicombe, the fields (below) form a colourful patchwork.*

large and handsome Church of St Michael in the village of Stokenham. The best view of the church is to be had from the lane leading south out of the village. The route follows this uphill through woodland and fields to Widdicombe Ⓐ, a hamlet in the parkland around Widdicombe

THE WALK

STOKENHAM – TORCROSS – SLAPTON SANDS

The walk begins just below Stokenham's church.

1 ➡ Walk away from the church towards the A379. Cross and go up the lane opposite and to your left, by the entrance to Stokenham House. Bear left, uphill, to a T-junction. Go straight across and through a rickety kissing-gate in the hedge. Go straight up the hill. With the fence and woods on your right, go through another kissing-gate.

2 ➡ After a few paces, turn left on a surfaced crossing track. Continue to a junction of paths ahead, with gateposts marked 'Private'. Turn left and follow the track through the hamlet of Widdicombe **A**. At Widdicombe Thatch, the path narrows and passes to the left of the cottage's garden. Continue on a narrow path down through the woods.

3 ➡ Where the trees end, cross two stiles and bear left around the drinking trough. Follow the broad track along the hedge-line to your right. Near the end of this large field, cross a stile half-hidden in the hedgerow, onto a narrow downhill path. At a crossing path, turn left (signposted to Torcross) and climb along a narrow,

House. This two-storey mansion was built around 1700.

The path is overhung with tree fuchsias, which are at their best in late spring and summer. As the path passes Widdicombe Thatch, the last in a row of fine cottages, it narrows, and descends through the centre of a strip of woodland. Widdicombe House can be glimpsed through the trees on your right.

As you emerge, you have your first view of the sea. In the foreground is a patchwork of red and green fields and a small, blue, fresh-water lagoon, Widdicombe Ley.

Beyond the resort of Beesands, the coast sweeps round and rises to the rocky headland of Start Point, which is topped by a gleaming white light-house. This acts as a landmark for migrating birds in spring and autumn, when ospreys can be seen en route to and from Scotland.

COASTAL PATH

Near the end of the pasture, half-hidden in the hedgerow, is a stile. A rocky, sometimes slippery path leads down from here, then begins a long, steady ascent. This cool, ferny corridor — a tunnel in summer when the greenery arches overhead — is part of the South Devon Coast

◄ *Widdicombe Ley and Beesands. Local fishermen once made crab-pots from osiers growing around the lagoon.*

RAY GRANGER

sometimes rocky path **B**, between trees, ferns and bracken. (Take special care of children and dogs near the quarry here.) At the top, continue on a wide green track to a wooden gate. Cross the field beyond, following a line of posts to another gate. Go through, then downhill on a winding path past houses. At a T-junction with a road, turn right and continue downhill into Torcross **C**. Turn right then left onto the sea front. At the end of the buildings, turn left and cross the road to the tank memorial **D** in a car park.

4 From the far end of the car park, continue on a footpath between the road and Slapton Ley **E** for 1½ miles (2.4km). At the end of the mere, turn left on the road to Slapton. Go over the bridge, then turn left down a signposted footpath through a wooden gate. Follow the nature trail **F** by the water's edge, up and down steps, and over stiles and bridges. At a fingerpost, continue ahead (signposted 'Slapton Village'). Follow the track as it bears round to the right to a wooden gate.

5 Do not go through, but turn left and follow a duckboard walk over the marsh. At the end, turn left on the path signposted to Deer Bridge. Continue along the lane to a road.

6 Turn left over the bridge. Bear left at the junction, up the hill, past Slapton Castle **G**, then walk along a lane between high hedgerows.

7 Just past Frittiscombe Lodge, turn sharp left down Frittiscombe Lane. Follow this quiet lane uphill then down again to a T-junction. Turn right then immediately sharp left, down the hill into the village of Stokenham **H**. At the next T-junction, turn left (with The Tradesman's Arms on your right). Bear right past the church to return to the start.

ALL PHOTOS: RAY GRANGER

▲ *The sea is visible from gaps in the high banks of lanes near Frittiscombe.*

▲ *Some short, muddy sections of the nature walk along the banks of the Ley are planked, while a long boardwalk (left) takes you through the centre of the lush vegetation of the marsh.*

Path **B**, which is followed on the next section of the walk.

You emerge into the light at the top of the climb. On your right, behind a stone wall covered with ivy and ivy-leaved toadflax, is an old quarry. Beyond this, the path goes through open pasture, with long views ahead along the curve of Start Bay to Combe Point at the mouth of the River Dart.

The route descends to the small resort of Torcross **C**. This was once a coach stop on a toll road along Slapton Sands. The Sands is actually a shingle ridge, made up mainly of flint and quartz, that runs ahead for over 3 miles (4.8km). It was created by tidal action since the sea level rose at the end of the last Ice Age.

The soil is thin, but supports a variety of plants, including gorse, campion, the daisy-like sea mayweed, yellow horned poppy, sea radish and wild carrot. In World War II, the beach was used for training exercises, and was the scene of a major disaster, commemorated by an unusual memorial **D** (see box).

NATURE TRAIL

The ridge has trapped a freshwater lagoon, Slapton Ley **E**, behind it. This is an important wildfowl habitat, and unusual in Devon. Ducks, grebes, geese and moorhens breed on the Ley, and dozens of species of migrating birds make landfall here in the spring and autumn.

▶ *Stokenham, where the walk begins and ends, is a charming village of whitewashed houses with two pubs.*

The walk turns inland to follow a well laid-out nature trail **F** around the shoreline. Across the water is France Wood, planted in the 19th century to provide oak for ship-building. A little inland, the route skirts Ireland Bay, 10 acres (4ha) of reed and marsh that are home to otters and shy birds such as reed warblers and water rails, as well as a roosting spot for hundreds of gulls.

MARSHES AND LANES

The trail crosses an inlet of lush marshland on duckboards, then heads up Marsh Lane, a track lined with trees and filled with darting electric blue and green damselflies and dragonflies. On Deer Bridge, you cross one of the four trickling streams that feed the Ley.

From here there is a steep climb up to Slapton Castle **G**, barely recognizable as a hill fort. Only a vestige of the banks that surrounded it remains. Its commanding hilltop position, however, can still be appreciated; there are long views to the north and east.

The route continues along a high-banked lane, with the occasional gate giving views back down to the sea, then turns off, down through the hamlet of Frittiscombe.

There is a final climb up another quiet lane, whose flowery banks attract many species of butterfly, before the descent into Stokenham **H**, which, in 1991, was voted the best-kept village in Devon. As you emerge above the church, by The Tradesman's Arms pub, there is a lovely row of white-painted, thatched cottages on your right.

BOTH PHOTOS: RAY GRANGER

Incident on the Sands

The Allied preparations for the invasion of France began in 1943. Beaches that resembled those to be used in the Normandy landings were commandeered for training. The shingle ridge of Slapton Sands was chosen to represent Utah Beach, where the US Army was to go ashore. Slapton village and much of the surrounding area was evacuated so that live ammunition exercises could take place. Many soldiers died in these rehearsals, known as Operation Tiger.

Then, on the night of 27 April 1944, German E-boats attacked some largely undefended landing ships in the Channel, and sank two of them before sailing away unscathed. In all, nearly

This amphibious Sherman tank was bought from the US government and raised from the sea by Ken Small, whose book, The Forgotten Dead, tells the story.

1,000 American servicemen, made up of 749 soldiers and the sailors crewing the landing ships, were killed. Many of the bodies were washed ashore near Torcross on the incoming tide. The actual landings on Utah Beach cost just 200 lives.

The disaster, known laconically in military histories as the Slapton Sands Incident, was kept secret, partly out of embarrassment but mainly to avoid giving the enemy any information about the invasion. The families of the dead men were told they had died in the D-Day landings six weeks later, on 6 June.

The story was told in 1946 in official military histories, but remained largely unknown for many years. A local man, Ken Small, wrote a book on the disaster and was responsible in 1984 for retrieving a rusting Sherman tank from the sea bed, where it had lain for 40 years. It was painted black and fixed on the shingle of Slapton Sands as a memorial to the men who died.

MIKE WILLIAMS. INSET: TOM LEACH/AQUILA

Explore a network of footpaths commanding magnificent views

▲*Torrington's South Commons rise steeply above the valley of the Torridge, crossed here by Taddiport Bridge. The emperor dragonfly (inset) hawks for insects up and down the river.*

Rising close to the source of the Tamar, the river Torridge twists and turns to reach the sea at Bideford. Its lush, wooded middle reaches, to the south-east of Great Torrington, were the setting for many scenes in Henry Williamson's classic, *Tarka the Otter* (see box on page 80). The river and the Commons that encircle two-thirds of the town bless Great Torrington with a rich range of wildlife habitats.

The Commons cover about 365 acres (148ha) and are latticed with over 20 miles (32km) of public paths and tracks of varying quality.

This walk follows some of the better routes. Soon after starting, you step through a stone arch and the land drops away almost 200 feet (60m), into a deep-gouged valley, through which the Torridge weaves like a languid serpent. Hedged fields clothe the humped hills ahead and thick woodland greens the valley sides. It is tempting to sit on a bench and stare, but there is much more to see further on.

The curtain wall here is Georgian, but stands on a castle site Ⓐ dating from Norman times. The last castle, built in 1340, was destroyed in the Civil War. A schoolhouse was built over the castle's chapel and is now the Eric Palmer Community Centre.

▼*There is a wonderful view over the valley very near the start of the walk.*

MIKE WILLIAMS

THE WALK

GREAT TORRINGTON – CADDYWELL – ROLLE BRIDGE

Start in the car park off South Street in Great Torrington.

1 Follow the old stone castle wall to the bottom left of the car park. Go down the steps and through an arch. Turn left across the site of the former castle **Ⓐ**, the wall to your left. Go straight on over a cross path, then fork right downhill. Follow the path as it winds down to the monument **Ⓑ**. With the monument on your right, turn left and continue downhill. Near the bottom, just past a side track, descend 10 wood-lipped steps to a path running parallel with the A386. After 150 yards (135m) the path joins the riverside track, once part of the Rolle Canal **Ⓒ**. Bear left and continue along the river to the main road.

2 Cross just before the road bridge, and head right. Go through the gateway to Mill Lodge (formerly Town Mills) **Ⓓ** and along the track, forking left after about 100 yards (90m) and skirting the edge of rhododendron woods. Turn left at the gate opposite Shallowford Lodge (Burwood Cottage on the map), onto the steep lane and follow it for about ½ mile (800m) to Caddywell.

3 On a right-hand bend, turn left on a lane by the old tannery **Ⓔ**. In 250 yards (225m), turn right on a marked steep track through the trees to the A386. Cross to the path opposite, walk on past the steps descended earlier and take the next small path to the left.

4 Follow this round to the right. The path becomes rocky as it approaches an outcrop, then drops to join the wider Rolle Road. Bear right and go straight on for about ½ mile (800m). Take the signed footpath left to Taddiport Bridge **Ⓕ**. Cross to the chapel **Ⓖ**, on the right, opposite the Post Office. Retrace your steps to the signpost.

5 Take the upper path on the left, in the same direction you came but at a higher level. Across the river are the narrow fields **Ⓗ** of the leper colony. Turn left into Popes Lane — a narrow tarmac lane bordered by stone walls between houses — and go ahead to Mill Street. Turn left, then right between numbers 84 and 86 up a concrete path to the common. Take the narrow path straight ahead. At a cross-path by a bench, go ahead, bearing slightly left to the top of the hill, where the path runs out.

6 Walk on, alongside the wall parallel to the road on the left, to the A386. Cross to the car park, bearing left across the old bowling green on the path on the extreme left, and continue for about 700 yards (630m) to the bottom of the hill.

7 Ignore the path joining sharp right. Follow a short tarmac section ahead and round to the right between iron posts to a stream. Cross by the footbridge and turn immediately hard right, then fork right on the grassy path next to the stream to a pond. Leave the pond up the wood-lipped steps, looking up on the left for two benches, past which the path ascends via more steps to join another path at the top. Turn right. Continue, taking the short fork right to cross Limer's Lane to a small path opposite, the start of Barmaid's Walk **Ⓙ**.

8 After ½ mile (800m), turn right, back on yourself, down wood-lipped steps (overgrown in summer) and a narrow gravelly path. Continue beside a stream past a ruined wooden bridge. Cross a footbridge and go up the steps on the other side, climbing steeply to emerge at an old stone wall fronting a line of majestic beeches. Keep the wall on the right.

9 When the wall ends, turn left and follow the wide, grassy track to a tarmac road at the rear of the Dartington Glass factory **Ⓚ**. Turn right into Stoneman's Lane and walk on to the junction with New Street.

10 Turn left. After 200 yards (180m), almost opposite Palmer House **Ⓛ** on the left, and before St Michael's Church **Ⓜ**, turn right into White's Lane. Turn left at the junction with South Street to return to the car park.

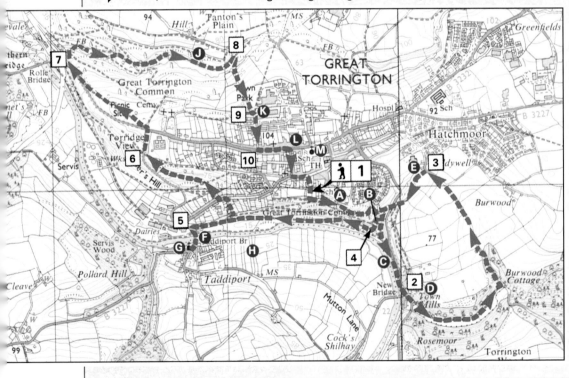

Nature Walk

THE ANATOMY OF THE OTTER

THE EARS flatten against the head when submerged, sealing the ear openings.
THE NOSTRILS are high on the nose to allow breathing when the rest of the body is submerged. They close automatically on diving.
WHISKERS on the mouth and forehead are sensitive enough to detect movement of fish in murky water, or at night.

COAT of thick hair traps a layer of air, which acts as a form of insulation.

TRACK of forefoot (right) is shorter than hindfoot; webbing gives unique appearance.

TAIL is extremely muscular; it is used both as a rudder and as a propeller when swimming.

PAWS have partial webbing for use in paddling; clawed fingers can grasp fish firmly.

PHIL WEARE/LINDEN ARTISTS

The path drops past the curious monument ❷ commemorating the Battle of Waterloo, and follows a sweeping bend in the river before squeezing tightly between the A386 on the left and the river on the right.

CANAL ROUTE

This section is part of the Rolle Road ❸, once the 7½ mile (12km) Rolle Canal, which was abandoned in 1870 due to competition from the new railway line from Bideford to Torrington. The canal's financier, Lord Rolle, also paid for New Bridge at Town Mills ❹. Once a water-powered grist mill, Town

ALL PHOTOS: MIKE WILLIAMS

Mills is perhaps best known as Tarka's hiding place when the final hunt gathered. Otters still live in the river, but are unlikely to be spotted by day as they are largely nocturnal.

Fine deciduous woods stand behind the mill. Tall silver birch reach for light in gaps in the heavy canopy of oak and ash near the stream. In the clearings, and by the woodland fringe tracks, you may see the dark green fritillary. Almost as big as a red admiral, it is one of the three largest British butterfly species. It flies in July and August but, like many other fritillaries, is becoming increasingly scarce.

Up the hill towards Caddywell, the route swings left at a modernized building. This was once a tannery ❺, and was situated deep in the open country due to the foul

▲A tall, attenuated pyramid above Town Mills commemorates the allies' victory over Napoleon at Waterloo.

◀This old stone building near the top of the hill in Caddywell was once a tannery, located well outside the town boundaries.

▼Also isolated, but for different reasons, was Taddiport Chapel, which was used by the leper colony that settled here in the Middle Ages.

stench of the pits of dogs' excrement used in the tanning process. An old, local saying suggested that you could smell a tanner long before you could see him.

UNUSUAL BRIDGE

From here, you head back along the Torridge all the way to Taddiport Bridge ❻. Look out for dragonflies here, particularly the largest British species, the emperor. The present 17th-century stone bridge is unusual

Tarka the Otter

Torrington is the heart of 'Tarka Country', the setting of Henry Williamson's novel *Tarka the Otter*. The book revolves around the sad but true story of the pursuit of an otter that Williamson raised from a cub. Published in 1927, it has become established as one of the best-loved pieces of nature writing in English. It is a superb evocation of the locality; many of the places it describes are largely unchanged.

Williamson himself hunted otters; the final hunt described in *Tarka* is said to be based on a memorable 10-hour hunt that took place in 1905. However, he grew to hate the sport and the people associated with it.

Henry Williamson was born in Bedfordshire in 1895, served on the Western Front during World War I and worked briefly as a freelance journalist in London. He then moved to Exmoor with his wife and began writing his first novel, *The Beautiful Years*, published in 1921.

Williamson had to wrestle with his publisher over some of the more esoteric material in *Tarka the Otter*. He wanted it left uncut; the publisher feared its popular appeal would be reduced. The battle cost the author dear in terms of his health and outlook, but he got his way. Williamson's book won the Hawthornden Prize, and his lasting fame was ensured.

Tarka's descendants and spirit live on today, helped both by the banning of otter hunting in the 1950s and by the continuation of Williamson's vision in projects such as The Tarka Trail, which is based in the Eric Palmer Centre, Great Torrington.

Though otters have not been hunted for many years, their populations are still falling in many areas due to loss of habitat.

▲ *There are good views back from the Commons of the lepers' strip fields.*

in that all the stone blocks have their longest sides placed vertically rather than horizontally. There has been a bridge here since at least the 13th century; it once gave access to a leper hospital on the opposite bank.

The little chapel of St Mary Magdalen ❻ was used by the lepers; a stained glass window from later years is inscribed in their memory. The colony farmed its own land; two of its strip fields ❽ can be seen after leaving the bridge on the ascent towards Torridge View.

BARMAID'S WALK

The walk continues through the town's western limits to the high Commons. An unmarked section, known as Barmaid's Walk ❿, is said to be the well-trodden route taken by a Victorian barmaid and her many gentlemen friends!

Returning to the town, the path emerges at the rear of the factory which produces Dartington Glass ❹. Free tours around the factory to see glass being blown and cut can be taken during the summer months.

The heart of the town is worth walking in its own right. Palmer House ❶ in New Street was built for a three-times Mayor of Torrington, John Palmer. He was the brother-in-law of Sir Joshua Reynolds, the portrait painter, and both he and Samuel Johnson stayed here.

Close by is St Michael's Church ⓜ. Thomas Wolsey, later Archbishop of Canterbury, was appointed rector here by Henry VIII. The town suffered badly in the Civil War, and St Michael's was accidently blown up in 1646, killing 200 Royalist prisoners held inside. The church was rebuilt in 1651 and restored in the mid-19th century, though parts of the original still stand.

▼ *These crenellated buildings at Town Mills, which features in* **Tarka the Otter,** *are now idiosyncratic holiday flats.*

A TINNER'S TRAIL

Industrial and prehistoric remains in wild moorland scenery

▲ *Only a few stones remain of the upper tin blowing mill at Yealm Steps. The keeled skimmer (below) flies by the River Yealm. The male has a blue abdomen; that of the female is yellow.*

PAUL STERRY/NATURE PHOTOGRAPHERS

TOM GREEVES

Southern Dartmoor is a human and natural landscape of extraordinary richness, where buzzards, ravens and herons are all likely to be seen. The fine scenery — the Rivers Yealm and Erme are especially beautiful — is dotted with remarkable prehistoric stone rows, circles and settlements, and there is extensive evidence of medieval tinworks and mills, where ore was crushed and smelted.

RING OF HUTS

The prehistoric enclosure **A** not far from the start is typical of many on Dartmoor. It probably dates from about 1500BC. A ruined wall contains within it the foundations of several circular houses with internal diameters of 16-23 feet (4.8-7m).

The remains of 5,000 such huts litter the moor. The walls would orginally have been 4-5 feet (1.2-1.5m) high and have supported a conical roof of light timbers covered

with heather, bracken or turf.

The Ranny Brook **B**, like just about every other Dartmoor stream, has been extensively worked for tin, as the heaps of stony waste indicate. A tinworks was documented here in the early 17th century, but some of the excavations are likely to be much earlier in date.

At Yealm Steps are the ruins of two mills **C** where tin was smelted (or 'blown'), probably in the 16th

and 17th centuries. Each blowing mill had a water-wheel operating the furnace bellows, and the moulds into which the molten tin was poured to make ingots can still be seen lying around the site.

The lower mill was noted in 1844, when it was mistakenly identified as a hermitage. This mill features in a romantic novel, *Guavas the Tinner*, published in 1897, by Sabine Baring-Gould (perhaps best known as the writer of *Onward Christian Soldiers*). Set in the 16th century, the novel explores the rivalry between Cornish and Devonian tinners.

THE DANCERS

The book also features the stone circle **D** a mile (1.6km) to the east. Known as 'The Dancers' or 'Kiss-in-the-Ring', it is beautifully sited on a gentle rise, and may date from about 2500BC. It marks the southern end of an amazing stone row that runs north for over 2 miles (3.2km), the longest of more than 70 stone rows known on Dartmoor. The circle is about 50 feet (15m) in diameter. You follow the row for a way, then cut off down a side valley to the Erme.

FACT FILE

❋ New Waste, 3 miles (4.8km) north of Ivybridge

▣ Outdoor Leisure Map 28, grid reference SX 625610

```
miles 0   1   2   3   4   5   6   7   8   9   10 miles
kms   0 1 2 3 4 5 6 7 8 9 10 11 12 13 14 15 kms
```

◔ Allow 5 to 6 hours

▲ Excellent rough moorland walking, with few defined paths and one steep gradient. Wear walking boots or stout shoes and take a compass, waterproofs and food. Do not attempt the walk when rivers and streams are in flood

Ⓟ Free parking for 6-8 cars at the start

⊞ None on the route. Pub and
Ⓧ shop in Cornwood, 1½ miles (2.4km) south-west of the start

THE WALK

NEW WASTE – STALLDOWN

To reach the start, take the road from Cornwood signposted 'Torr and Harford'. At Torr, go left then almost immediately right. At a junction, bear left. Keep straight on for ½ mile (800m). Park just beyond the gate on the left.

1 ► Follow the signposted permissive path. After 600 yards (540m), you go through a gate onto the open moor. Keep the wall on your left until it veers away and starts dropping steeply downhill. Keep straight ahead to the outline of a ruined prehistoric enclosure wall **A** which straddles a stream (usually dry).

2 ► Bear left to follow the contour, bending right around the rise to the Ranny Brook **B**. Cross, and continue at the same level to the foot of Yealm Steps, and the remains of a tin blowing house **C**. Bear right up the river. Above the waterfall is another blowing house, on the opposite side. Go ahead for another 200 yards (180m).

3 ► Strike out right (north-east) over a gently rising hill, then descend to Bledge Brook. Cross at an old ford about 100 yards (90m) above the only group of trees on the stream. Bear slightly right (due east) on the contour to the prehistoric stone circle, The Dancers **D**.

4 ► Turn left. Follow the stone row for ½ mile (800m), to a steep side valley of the River Erme. Strike off right down to the Erme, and cross to another stream, Hook Lake, and

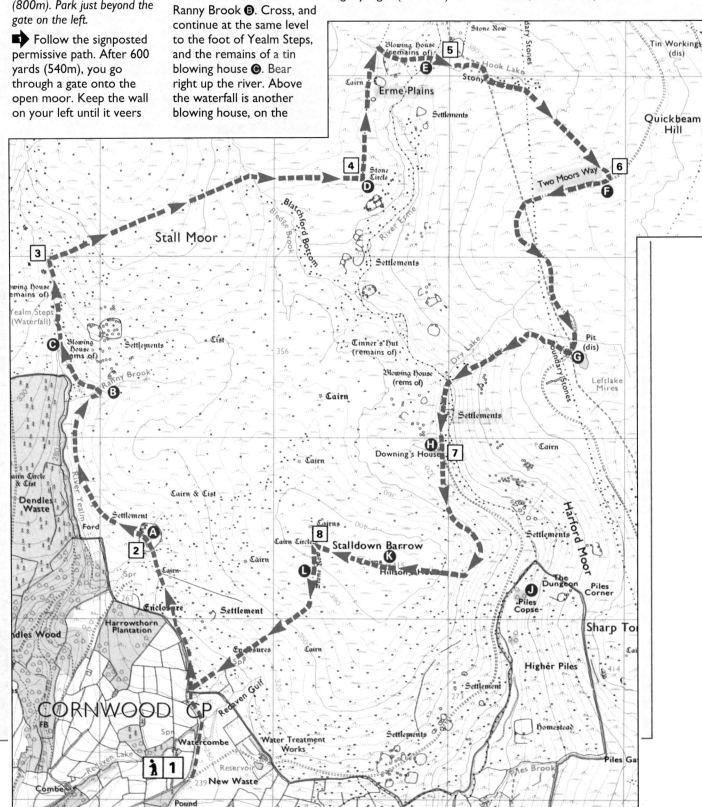

another ruined tin mill **E**.

5 Follow the stream on your right for about 250 yards (225m), through the tinworks, then cross it at an old ford. Follow the scarp edge of the tinworks upstream. Cross the line of boundary stones, then strike out half-right for about 650 yards (585m).

6 Turn right along the old tramway **F** to the disused Leftlake Clayworks **G**, then turn right down Left Lake stream to its junction with the Erme by a small reservoir. Cross the Erme, and follow a good track down to the first tributary valley to the ruins of Downing's House **H**.

7 Continue ahead up the steep slope of the hill, but keep on its flank to soften the climb and also to give views of Piles Copse **J** on the opposite side of the valley. Veer right for the final climb to Hillson's House **K**. Continue ahead (west) over the hilltop to the stones of the Stalldown prehistoric row **L**.

8 Turn left to follow the row down to its end, then bear half right down to the gate where you entered the moor. Return along the track to the start.

ALL PHOTOS: TOM GREEVES

▲*The mouldstone at the bottom of the picture was used to make tin ingots.*

At the very bottom of Hook Lake (from 'lacu', Old English for stream), is another ruined tinners' mill **E**, recorded in 1661. The dry leat, which once brought water to the mill-wheel, can be clearly seen on the north side, high above. Inside the mill is a curious slotted stone that once supported machinery for crushing ore. You follow the stream up through the extensive workings, then head off across the moor.

Further on is another remarkable industrial relic, a disused tramway **F**. Constructed in 1910-12, it carried men and materials for 8 miles (12.8km), from Bittaford, near Ivybridge, to the Red Lake china clay works to the north of Hook Lake. The conical waste tip at Red Lake is visible from several points of the walk. The works and tramway were abandond in 1932.

PIPELINE AND MOONSHINE

You follow the tramway to the clayworks at Leftlake **G**, which were first opened in the 1850s and reopened for a few years in 1922. Running beside the tramway are the remains of a pipeline that carried the clay, in solution, to treatment works.

On the other side of the Erme, is a small 'beehive' shelter, with a corbelled drystone roof, which is known as Downing's House **H**. One of the best preserved of its kind on Dartmoor, it is said to have been a place for concealing illicit liquor. It is probably the work of the tinners, and is actually constructed within the ruins of a larger building.

▲*From the top of Yealm Steps there is a good view of the way you have come. The stone circle known as The Dancers (below) was built around 2500BC.*

This is the beginning of the climb up Stalldown. Piles Copse **J**, which can be seen hugging the steep flank of Sharp Tor on the opposite side of the Erme, is one of three ancient woods, remnants of the original woodland covering Dartmoor. The trees are pedunculate oak.

On the top of Stalldown is a fine prehistoric cairn, a stony burial mound thought to be between 3,000 and 4,000 years old. Many hundreds of these cairns survive on Dartmoor. In the top of this one, the ruins of a substantially built rectangular

ALL PHOTOS: TOM GREEVES

Dartmoor Tin

The tin industry of Dartmoor has an 800-year-old history, from the 12th to the 20th century. Activity peaked in the 16th century, when several hundred tinworks were operating, as well as scores of water-powered mills for crushing and smelting the ore. Rich archaeological remains survive from all periods.

Tin occurs all over the granite mass of Dartmoor and in some of the surrounding rocks too. Deep shafts were in use by the 15th century, but the oldest method of recovering ore was stream-working,

a technique similar to gold panning. Tinstone was heavier than other minerals and so could be separated from impurities by washing.

All of the rivers on moorland Dartmoor show clear signs of having been turned over extensively by the tinners in their search for ore. Stony waste heaps are visible everywhere, sometimes with drystone retaining walls.

Small water-wheels drove ore-crushing machinery and the bellows that provided a forced draught for smelting. At many sites you can see mortarstones with two or three smoothly worn hollows. These are the stones on which the ore was crushed; they were abandoned once the hollows were worn too deep.

More rarely, you can find neat, rectangular troughs, or mouldstones. Molten tin was poured into them to make ingots which weighed as much as 200 pounds (90kg).

The tinner's life could be harsh. A late 16th-century account said that 'he goes so near the weather as no man can live more frugally or nearer than he does'. The tinners also had a notorious prison at Lydford which, in 1512, was described as 'one of the most annoious, contagious and detestable places wythin this realme'.

The last mine closed in November 1930, and now only the abandoned workings and ruined buildings bear witness to an ancient industrial tradition.

Molten tin was taken from the furnace and poured into mouldstones, such as this double one, to turn it into rectangular ingots.

▲*The tramway bridge and flooded claypit at Leftlake. Dartmoor ponies (below) drinking by the row of prehistoric stones on Stalldown.*

structure, known as Hillson's House **K**, are visible. According to a 19th-century legend, this was the house and workshop of a local clock-maker who had been discovered, abandoned, on this hill as a baby.

MARCHING MEGALITHS

The prehistoric stone row **L** on Stalldown is one of the finest on Dartmoor, with some truly massive stones. Four of the largest stones are visible from many points on the walk, and look like figures striding across the hilltop. Several cairns are associated with the row, but its purpose, like that of all others, remains a matter of speculation.

In fine, clear weather, there are spectacular views to be had to the south and west from this row, and as you descend back towards the start.

DAVID BUXTON. INSET: A. BARNES/NHPA

▲*Okehampton Castle was once the biggest fortification in Devon. The silver-washed fritillary (left) flies in the riverside woodland on the walk.*

A ramble through hills and woodland to a romantic ruin

Okehampton lies roughly at the midpoint between Exeter, the administrative capital of Devon, and Launceston, the ancient capital of Cornwall. It owes its importance to its strategic position on the main road route through the two counties, today's A30. Tucked below the tors marking the northern limits of Dartmoor, Okehampton has seen centuries of traffic pass through its pretty streets; its many pubs and hotels are testimony to that.

As cars increased in popularity, this traditional gateway to the south-west became a barrier to it; holiday traffic frequently choked the town to a standstill. Okehampton became a byword for bottlenecks. Now, the A30 has been re-routed so it bypasses the old town.

There is plenty to see and do in Okehampton before starting on the walk. The Museum of Dartmoor Life **A** has exhibits that reveal the fascinating relationship between the moor and those who made their home there in days gone by.

From the museum, it is just a short stroll to Town Mills **B**, on the edge of the town. Formerly a grist and woollen mill, it was still working in the 1950s, but is now private houses. However, the old mill-wheel still turns, driven by a leat from the East Okement River.

LIVELY STREAM

From the mill to the halfway point of the walk, the route never strays far from the little river, whose voice grows louder and more exuberant at each upstream stretch. Mixed woodland cloaks the valley sides; in August, the green is startlingly punctuated by the scarlet berries of rowan, or mountain ash.

Squirrels abound here, and nuthatches betray their presence by hammering on nuts wedged in tree bark, while furtive jays utter their harsh curses from a safe distance.

The imposing stone viaduct at Fatherford **C** has carried a railway for over a century. It is still used, but only to transport stone from a nearby quarry. Beyond the viaduct, the river and landscape become noticeably wilder as the path enters the upper valley **D** of the East Okement River. There used to be a variety of trees on the lower stretches, but now there are only widely spaced, moss-covered oaks. Great slabs of rock erupt along the valley sides.

The river is at its most splendid here, running fast and shallow, and noisy with gushing water. The climb out of the wood reveals a brief taste

▼*As you climb East Hill on a sunken lane, splendid views open up behind you over Lower Halstock, and beyond.*

DAVID BUXTON

THE WALK

OKEHAMPTON – LOWER HALSTOCK

The walk starts from the car park in Market Street, Okehampton.

1 Turn left out of the main entrance and walk along Market Street to West Street. Turn left, then immediately right into George Street. After 100 yards (90m), turn right into Jacob's Pool to the museum **A**. Return to George Street and continue walking along it, curving left. Town Mills **B** appears ahead on a bend.

2 Climb the concrete steps next to the water-wheel and turn right at the top. After 30 paces, turn right along a tarmac track signposted to Ball Hill and Father Ford. After 100 yards (90m), the track goes through a wooden gate onto a stony track signposted 'Ball Hill Footpath'. Follow this through two fields.

3 At the third kissing-gate, go straight ahead and enter the woodland through the 5-bar gate. Continue on the woodland path for just over ½ mile (800m) to a 5-bar gate by a small pumping station.

4 Beyond the gate, turn right onto a tarmac lane. Go through another gate and under Fatherford Viaduct **C**. Turn immediately right across a wooden footbridge over the river. After 10 paces, turn left through the 5-bar gate and go straight ahead under the A30. Follow the signposted path through the wooded upper valley **D** of the East Okement River for nearly a mile (1.6km), crossing a stream about halfway along. Where the path breaks right by waterfalls on your left, follow it up a steep fenced rocky slope to a three-way signpost, simply marked 'path', 'path' and 'path'.

5 Turn sharp right. You emerge at a gate. The path leads over bracken-covered slopes. Eventually it rounds a cottage to a gate.

6 Turn right towards the farmyard gate ahead. A bridleway sign points you through Lower Halstock's farmyard, onto the surfaced drive. Walk along this to a road.

7 Turn right. Follow the road over a road-bridge and a railway bridge.

8 Opposite a nursing home on your right, take the path through a kissing-gate on your left (signposted for Okehampton Castle). Where the path joins a tarmac drive, keep ahead. After 100 yards (90m), turn sharp right up the signposted path. You cross the river and emerge at a car park.

9 To visit the castle **E**, turn left out of the car park. Otherwise, turn right onto a road over the river. After ¼ mile (400m), turn left on St Georges Road. Bear left at the end and retrace the way you came earlier, back to the start.

---

of the delicious panoramas to come, as the path opens to cross the bracken-covered slopes towards Lower Halstock Farm.

A made-up track presents you with a long, gentle ascent to the highest point on the walk. From this open shoulder of the moorland edge, the views to the left, right and ahead are limited only by the light.

The return route is downhill all the way. Beyond the bridges over

▶ *The walk follows the East Okement River as it passes through woodland and bubbles and foams noisily over rocks.*

DAVID BUXTON

the A30 and the railway, the keep of Okehampton Castle **E** peeks over the trees, as yet giving no sign that it was part of Devon's largest castle.

ROYAL DISFAVOUR

The Norman castle was begun by Baldwin de Brionne, but most of it dates from a reconstruction in the early 1300s. In 1538, Henry VIII had the owner, Lord Exeter, beheaded and partly dismantled his castle.

Close to the castle, the route crosses the West Okement River, on its way to meet the East Okement, and returns to the centre of town.

MIKE WILLIAMS. INSET: PAUL STERRY/NATURE PHOTOGRAPHERS

architectural delights of one of the finest small towns in England. The broad street called The Plains opens to the left, bounded on one side by carefully converted warehouses and on the other by elegantly restored Georgian buildings.

The openness of The Plains is in sharp contrast to narrow Fore Street, which rises steeply through the heart of the town. The small shops lining this street are discreetly built

◀ *The car park where the walk starts overlooks the waters at Steamer Quay, which provide moorings for pleasure boats. The buff ermine moth (inset) thrives on the damp conditions hereabouts. This fine Gothic building off Fore Street (below), complete with battlements, is used as an art gallery.*

MIKE WILLIAMS

FACT FILE

- ☀ Totnes, 5 miles (8km) west of Torbay, on the A385

- 🗺 Outdoor Leisure Map 20 and Pathfinder 1341 (SX 76/77), grid reference SX 806599

  miles 0 1 2 3 4 5 6 7 8 9 10 miles
  kms 0 1 2 3 4 5 6 7 8 9 10 11 12 13 14 15 kms

- ◔ Allow at least 2½ hours

- ▬ The town section includes a steep climb up Fore Street. A long climb up Harper's Hill; Coplands Lane is very wet and muddy after rain

- P Long-stay car park at the start (fee payable)

- T Totnes is on the main London-Plymouth BR line. Buses from most South Devon towns. Regular boat services from Dartmouth

- 🍴 Several pubs, restaurants, cafés and tea-rooms in Totnes

- WC At start; three others in town

- I For tourist information, including details of Totnes Castle, Tel. (01803) 863168

Architectural delights and old lanes in a period-piece town

Totnes can surprise the visitor from the start. This is the lowest crossing point of the tidal River Dart, but it is not particularly wide, and does not look very deep. Yet high water brings ocean-going ships upriver to the town's doorstep. Opposite Steamer Quay, where the walk begins, large freighters can be seen unloading cargoes of timber. This is not an industrial scene, though; no docks blight the waterfront, and the commercial activity blends easily with the leisure craft and passenger cruisers that ply regularly between Totnes and Dartmouth.

MOTOR MUSEUM

Further up Steamer Quay is Totnes Motor Museum ❹, where vintage, sports and racing cars of famous international marques form the backbone of an exhibition covering eight decades of motoring.

Crossing Totnes Bridge brings you the first glimpse of the many

into the frontages of the old buildings. A timbered top storey overhangs the bottom one; and it is always worthwhile looking up at the top storeys to see intriguing architectural details.

The arch of the East Gate ❺, the town's best known landmark, straddles the street near the top of the rise. This medieval gateway was almost lost in 1990 when fire, traditionally a scourge in Totnes's close-packed streets, caused serious damage. The gateway has now been

THE WALK

TOTNES

The walk begins at the car park at Steamer Quay.

1 With the river on your left, follow the quayside, then turn left along Steamer Quay Road. Pass the motor museum **A** and turn left at the T-junction.

2 At the next T-junction, turn left and cross Totnes Bridge. At the mini-roundabout, go to the left of the Royal Seven Stars Hotel. Walk up Fore Street to the East Gate **B**.

3 Turn right into Guildhall Yard, directly under the arch, climbing two flights of stone steps. Turn left into the churchyard of St Mary's **C**. Follow the path around the church to the opposite side, passing one gate and turning left through the next, to emerge in front of the guildhall **D**.

4 Turn left out of the church gate and left again into a narrow alley. Turn right into the High Street ahead. Follow the road as it narrows and curves left. Where the main route swings right, keep straight ahead (with the Bull Inn on your left) to the junction with the main road (Totnes Bypass) at the top.

5 Cross to the lane opposite, marked 'Harper's Hill Unsuitable for Motors', and follow it to a junction at the top of the hill.

6 Turn right. After ½ mile (800m), turn right down the unmarked track that drops away in front of a small clump of trees that form a high hedge. Fork right near the bottom.

Continue to a crossroads. Go ahead on the road opposite, and cross the railway bridge. The road rises.

7 At the top, turn right through a break in the hedgerow along a muddy, overgrown green lane. Continue for about ¾ mile (1.2km) to a junction with a new road and housing development (not shown on the map). Bear right to another junction, then turn right. Continue to a T-junction with a main road.

8 Cross, bear left and turn almost immediately right into Malt Mill. Go under the railway bridge and turn left. Keep on the right of the road. With The Globe pub on your left, bear right into Castle Street.

9 After a few paces, turn sharp right up a narrow tarmac path between high walls. Keep ahead into Castle Street. Go under a stone arch, then turn sharp right up a tiny rising path to Totnes Castle **E**. Return to Castle Street and continue to a T-junction. Turn left into the High Street and retrace your steps across the bridge to the start.

MIKE WILLIAMS

fully restored, at vast expense.

Just off Fore Street, beyond the East Gate, is the Church of St Mary **C**. Its unusually red sandstone is almost incandescent on a bright day. The stone rood screen inside is one of the finest in Britain.

◀A view over the skyline of Totnes to the squat, circular castle keep.

Beside the church stands the guildhall **D**, on the site of the refectory of an 11th-century Benedictine priory dedicated to St Mary. The town's mayors have been chosen here for over 400 years.

QUIET LANES

As you head away from the centre, the narrow street closes in still further. A bypass marks the boundary of the built-up area; crossing it marks a sudden break. Only a few strides into Harper's Hill, the hubbub fades to silence. The tarmac lane gives way to a broken, stony track, which rises relentlessly for ½ mile (800m) over Windmill Down. Until the mid-18th century, this lonely green lane was the Plymouth road.

From the top of the hill, Dartmoor fills the horizon to the distant north and west. Here and there, where the arable land has been freshly broken, patches of rich red earth show through against the green.

The return to town is along another old lane. Copland Lane is often wet and overgrown; clumps of great plantain cover the ground around pools of standing water.

Totnes Castle **E** lies at the end of the walk's circuit. The 15-foot-thick (4.5-m) walls of its circular keep are remarkably intact, largely because no serious battles took place here. As a viewpoint over the town and the surrounding area, though, the castle is as dominant as it ever was. It is open to the public during the summer and there is no better place from which to survey Totnes before returning to the start.

MILTON ABBAS

Through beautiful Dorset, from an 18th-century village to an ancient abbey

This walk in the glorious Dorset countryside centres around a model village, built by an unscrupulous landowner, and a 14th-century abbey set in a beautiful landscape created by 'Capability' Brown.

GRAND PLAN

The recent history of Milton Abbey **C** and the village of Milton Abbas **A** are inextricably linked by the deeds of an 18th-century landowner. This man was Joseph Damer, who later became Lord Milton, Earl of Dorchester. An

JON PRATTY

JON PRATTY. INSET: STEPHEN DALTON/NHPA

▲ *A view of Milton Abbey Church, glimpsed through trees. The parkland woods provide ideal nesting for the Little Owl (inset). Grassy steps (left) lead to St Catherine's Chapel. Legend has it that Athelstan camped on the ridge above, en route to fight the Danes.*

unpopular landlord, Damer was regarded as selfish and unscrupulous. Horace Walpole described him as excessively proud and arrogant, the only basis for this being his great wealth and his marriage to the Duke of Dorset's daughter.

The original town of Milton was set on the southern side of the Abbey. As part of his grand plan for his estate, Damer resolved to erase the town from his back door and re-house its people in a new village, out of sight and a mile away.

Although all the power lay in the hands of Lord Milton, many of the villagers resisted and it took 20 years for him to realise his ambition. The town's grammar school also proved a problem for Damer. In order to have it removed, a Parliamentary Bill was required, but the resourceful Damer succeeded in achieving this at only his second attempt. It seems that his chief complaint was the behaviour of the boys who stole his apples, threw bricks down his chimneys and engaged in cockfighting. One of the ringleaders of this unruly group is said to have

FACT FILE

- ☀ Milton Abbas
- ▭ Pathfinders 1300 (ST80/90) and 1299 (ST60/70), grid reference ST806018

  miles 0 1 2 3 4 5 6 7 8 9 10 miles
  kms 0 1 2 3 4 5 6 7 8 9 10 11 12 13 14 15 kms

- ◔ Allow 2 hours for short walk, 3 hours for longer walk
- ▬ One steep climb for about 100 yards (90 metres) mainly through fields. Good walking shoes recommended
- P At roadside in Milton Abbas
- 🏠 Pub food in Milton Abbas, refreshments at Milton Farm Park Museum.
- WC Toilets in Milton Abbey grounds

THE WALK

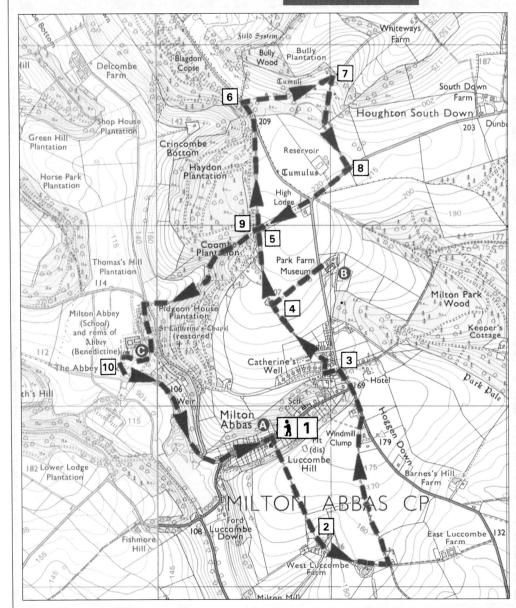

MILTON ABBAS – MILTON ABBEY

The walk begins in Milton Abbas village, close to the church.

▶1 Take the path sign-posted between the church and the gift shop in Milton Abbas **A**. Walk up the hill with churchyard on your right. Pass through a small wood to a waymarked stile. Climb this stile and cross the field to another stile directly in front of you. Climb this second stile and follow another waymarked arrow, up and across the field in front of you. The way is marked at the corner of a field that leads you down to West Luccombe Farm.

▶2 A yellow arrow will direct you through a metal gate, straight ahead and down a bank to another way-marked gate beside a metal barn. Go through the gate and turn left. Walk straight ahead past a building on supports on your right and up a track. At the top of the rise go past some farm buildings on your right and, just before you reach a house, turn left up a track beside a metal six-bar gate.

Milton Abbas, with its rows of neat cottages, has all the appearance of a well-planned village.

been Thomas Masterman Hardy, later Lord Nelson's Flag Captain.

Milton Abbey comprised two main buildings, the Abbey Church and the Abbey House. The beautiful Abbey Church dates from the 14th and 15th centuries (although legend has it that the original church was founded by King Athelstan in AD 934 after he had a vision that he would defeat the Danes in a coming battle). In 1309 the original wooden abbey was struck by lightning and destroyed in the resulting fire. In 1331 building began on the present Abbey Church and continued up to the Dissolution in 1539.

The Abbey buildings were granted to Sir John Tregonwell by Henry VIII. The rebuilding of the church was never completed, prevented, it is thought, by plague.

In 1752 Joseph Damer bought the estates from the Tregonwell family. He demolished all the monastic buildings except for Abbot's Hall, which was incorporated in the new building.

LEGENDARY PAST

One of the most outstanding architects of the 18th century, Sir William Chambers, was commissioned to design the new Milton Abbey mansion. True to form, Milton quarrelled with Chambers over payment of fees and replaced him with James Wyatt who complet-

You are now walking in a northerly direction. Ahead is a hedge on your right.

Climb over a wooden three-bar railed fence (waymarked) and continue along the next field with a hedge on your right. Just as Hill House comes into view, note a gate and a path to the road on your right. At the road go left. At the T-junction ignore the Milton Abbas signs and go straight on. You pass Hill House, now the Milton Manor Hotel.

3 Turn left down Catherine's Well opposite a sign indicating 'Forestry Commission Private Road'. Just before a shallow crescent of houses, turn right up a grass path between a fence and hedge and into a children's play area. Go left through the play area and, just before the garages straight in front of you, is a gate with a blue waymark labelled 'Bridleway'. Go through the gate and follow the path over the field to the next gate. Follow the path along the edge of the next field keeping the mature hedge to your left.

4 There is a track going right following a line of telephone poles. If you want to go to Milton Park Farm Museum **B**, take this track. At the road turn right and then left into the Museum.

After visiting the Farm Museum, retrace your steps and carry on up the bridlepath with the hedge to your left. This changes to a wall and the path goes left out of the field to walk between a row of conifers and the hedge. Go through three more gates and past well-kept gardens on your left until you reach a gravel track.

5 For those wishing to take the shorter walk, go to Stage 9. For the longer walk turn right, walk up the track for 50 yards (45 metres), then turn left around the top of the tennis court and go diagonally with a fruit cage on your left to the side of Coombe Plantation.

Continue northwards and go through a wooden gate in a barbed wire fence. The bridleway is clearly delineated at this stage with a barbed wire fence and the plantation on your left and an electric fence on your right.

Go past some far sheds, through another wooden gate and out on to the road (in summer, the path may be densely grown with nettles). Walk straight on down this road with a small group of hazelnut trees on your right.

6 At the end of the group of hazel trees, and within 200 yards (180 metres), turn right through a wooden gate. Here there is a blue waymark. Walk out on to the field for the village of Winterborne Houghton, which nestles in the valley in front of you.

Continue walking along the top of the slope, slightly to the right, and, with the pylon in the middle distance in view, gradually drop down towards some woods.

7 Go down towards a waymarked post and two metal gates in the corner of the field. Do not go out of the field but turn sharp right and follow the clear tracks up the hill. Follow the track, which becomes less clear to the top of the field and a six-bar metal gate. Go through the gate and follow the track straight on to the road.

8 At the road, turn right. At the junction, go straight on between the ornamental pillars and past a red-roofed bungalow on your right. This track takes you to Coombe Plantation.

9 Go through the metal gates of the gatehouse and take the path straight in front of you, which goes down through Coombe Plantation, alongside Pidgeon House Plantation and to Milton Abbey **C**. The path through laurel trees gradually widens. Eventually you will see the playing fields of Milton Abbey School. A field and a metal fence appear on your right and Pidgeon House Plantation to your left. At the road go left into the school grounds.

10 After visiting the Abbey make your way back to the village of Milton Abbas. Follow the track from the school area near the hockey courts and continue along a well-defined path with a sturdy wooden fence on your right and a hilly ridge on your left. The path also follows the course of the stream that feeds the lake, part of Lancelot 'Capability' Brown's natural landscaping of the area.

On this final leg of the walk you are moving through the last trace of the original town of Milton.

▲ *The brick-and-flint Tregonwell Almshouses, in the centre of the village, are replicas of the 17th-century houses in the original village.*

▶ *The rural museum at Milton Park Farm displays old farm implements.*

ed the work. The mansion is now used as a school but is open to the public during school holidays.

On the hill to the east of the Abbey buildings stands St Catherine's Chapel, which was originally erected by Athelston. Although 100 grass steps lead up to it, these are now closed to the public and the chapel can be reached by road.

The only surviving dwelling of the old town is a delightful 15th-century Green Walk Cottage close by the grass steps. Its lone survival serves as a poignant reminder of the extent of Damer's selfish vandalism.

Stunning views over Crincombe Bottom, reveal the full beauty of the Dorset countryside.

On seeing Milton Abbey village today, it is hard to believe that it was able to accommodate all of the families uprooted from the original town. It must be remembered, however, that this process took 20 years to engineer and that many people will have moved out of the district during that time.

THE NEW VILLAGE

The village was designed to cater for the basic needs of the villagers and the provision included a church and vicarage, a brewery and inn, a blacksmith's forge, a bakery, a dairy and almshouses. Most of the cottages in the new village are in identical pairs on either side of the road, thatched and white-rendered. They are equally spaced and lie back from the road behind large well-tended and regular lawns.

In the centre of the village stand the brick-and-flint almshouses (charity houses) opposite the 18th-century church of St James.

Park Farm Museum **B**, labelled Milton Park Farm on the map, is a good place to break your walk for a picnic whilst admiring unforgettable Dorset. There are numerous farm animals including pigs, calves, horses, donkeys, rabbits, guinea pigs, goats, sheep, chickens and dogs. Children are encouraged into the pens to touch and stroke the animals.

The museum is housed in thatched former stables and holds an extensive collection of rural farm implements and domestic tools. The curiosities include the Reverend Fletcher's unique collection of chimney pots. For the children there are pony and tractor rides and a play area. The owners claim you can see the coast from the garden (on a clear day, of course).

Lancelot Capability Brown

The landscape gardener who designed the estate of Milton Abbey and selected the setting for the new model village revolutionized the layout of gardens and parklands in the 18th century. He opened the eyes of the world to the beauties of the natural landscape by creating a setting which appeared unplanned, using hills, scattered groups of trees and serpentine lakes. His habit of saying, on viewing a new site, 'I see great capability of improvement here', gave rise to his famous nickname.

Brown was born in 1716 in the Northumberland hamlet of Kirkharle, the fifth child of a family of yeomen stock. He stayed at school until he was 16, and was then employed by the local landowner to work in his kitchen garden. At the age of 23, he moved south to Buckinghamshire to work for relations of his former employer. Two years later he moved to Stowe where he stayed for over 10 years, and progressed from head gardener to qualified architect. During his time at Stowe he made many contacts, which were to prove invaluable in his later career.

For the next 30 years Brown was extremely busy laying out the estates of great houses. The list of his commissions covers the whole of England from Northumberland to Kent and reads like a touring guide to the greatest gardens in the land — Harewood, Chatsworth, Longleat, Broadlands, Blenheim, Prior Park, Bowood, Syon House, Hampton Court and many others.

The revolutionary ideas of Capability Brown (inset) transformed English garden design in the 18th century. The river walk in Milton Abbey park (below) shows the naturalistic effect of his work.

92

DORSET

DEREK FORSS. INSET: JOHN HAYWOD/NHPA

Across heathland and along the coast south of Studland Bay

The village of Studland **Ⓐ** is located in an area called the Isle of Purbeck. This is not an island but part of the Dorset countryside, bounded by the English Channel to the south and east, by Poole Harbour and the River Frome to the north, and by the stream called Luckford Lake to the west.

CHALK HILLS

As a result of its underlying geology, the area may be divided into four natural regions each running from west to east. In the north is a relatively level area of heathland on the Bagshot beds. To the south of this is a long narrow ridge of chalk called the Purbeck Hills. Then there is a valley of Wealden clay. Finally there is an upland area of Purbeck and Portland beds that presents a

FACT FILE

☀ Studland, 3 miles (5 km) north of Swanage on the B3351

🗺 Outdoor Leisure Map 15, grid reference SZ 038825

miles 0 | 1 | 2 | 3 | 4 | 5 | 6 | 7 | 8 | 9 | 10 miles
kms 0 | 1 | 2 | 3 | 4 | 5 | 6 | 7 | 8 | 9 | 10 | 11 | 12 | 13 | 14 | 15 kms

🕐 Allow 4 hours

▬ Parts of the route can become muddy and boots are recommended

🅿 In Studland

🚌 Buses from Bournemouth and Swanage

🍴 The Bankes Arms Hotel. Café
🍴 on the beach to the north of Redend Point, which is open in the summer and on winter weekends

🚾 Near the beginning and end of the walk

▲*Old Harry is a broad chalk stack, standing between Studland Bay and Swanage Bay. Wild flowers grow on the clifftops, such as the Dorset Heath (inset), which flowers in August.*

rocky coastline to the south. This walk combines the sombre beauty of the heath with the more dramatic beauty of the Purbeck Hills.

In 1982 some of the most beautiful scenery in the county was bequeathed to the National Trust. This gift included Studland Heath, Ballard Down and part of the south coast of Purbeck.

SPACESHIP EARTH

Studland is noted for its church, the interior of which retains many Norman features, including two rib-vaulted ceilings. To the south of the church is a stone cross bearing the inscription 'Spaceship Earth' and the date 1976.

The most remarkable building in the village is its manor house, which is embellished with an enormous

THE WALK

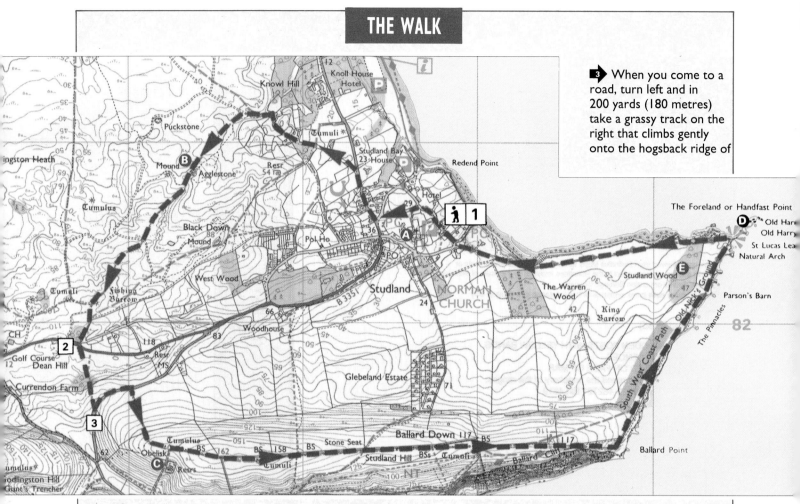

When you come to a road, turn left and in 200 yards (180 metres) take a grassy track on the right that climbs gently onto the hogsback ridge of

STUDLAND - BALLARD DOWN

The walk begins at the South Beach car park adjoining the Bankes Arms in Studland **A**.

1 Turn left out of the car park and continue along the road to a junction and go left. At the end of the road turn left and immediately right following sign to toll ferry. In about ¼ mile (400 metres) turn left into Wadmore Lane. The lane narrows to a path that enters a wood and crosses over a footbridge. Bear left and continue on sandy path through wood. Leave the wood and after 50 yards (30 metres) take a path on the left and follow it across the heath to the Agglestone **B**. Walk round the left-hand side of the Agglestone and continue on the main path that bears slightly to the right. The path forks at a National Trust sign. Take the right fork and follow the blue arrows over a golf course to the Studland road. (Beware of flying golf balls.)

2 Cross the road and continue over a stile where a pointed piece of wood indicates the direction to be taken. At the far side of the golf course, pass to the right of a derelict building and cut down through the woodland to a stile where the route is indicated by a yellow arrow.

Ballard Down. You will shortly pass the obelisk **C**. Stay on the ridge until it reaches the sea and then follow the coastal footpath to the left. At Handfast Point, from where you will get the closest view of Old Harry **D**, the path bends left and passes along the edge of Studland Wood **E**. After ¾ mile (1.25 km) bear right along a path to Studland. When you reach the road, turn right to the Bankes Arms.

number of tiny stone-roofed gables.

Extending to the north from the village to the mouth of Poole Harbour is a magnificent sandy beach backed by sand dunes. Behind the dunes is the lake called the Little Sea which was joined to the sea until 1850. On the shore of the lake are hides for bird watching. Poole Harbour itself is a large natural inlet that is linked to the sea by a narrow entrance only ¼ mile (400 metres) wide. The shore is fringed with sea lavender. Sea purslane grows along the margins of creeks, while further out the mud flats are covered in rice grass.

ISLAND LIFE

The only island of any size in Poole harbour is Brownsea Island, where red squirrels are found and where the first Boy Scout camp was held in 1907. There are also Round Island, where Sir Thomas Beecham wrote the biography of Delius; Long Island, which was used as a hideout by Harry Paye the pirate, Green Island, which was formerly used as a pottery and Furzey Island, which is now used for the extraction of oil.

In the Middle Ages, the Isle of Purbeck was an important source of

◄Studland's Norman church of St Nicholas of Myra has not been restored and remains unspoiled.

▼Legendary explanations of the origins of the Agglestone include the Devil carrying it from the Isle of Wight.

with the sun so that it does not cast a shadow, and the silver-studded blue (hard to distinguish from the common blue). The silver-studded blue is most often seen in July; the grayling in late July and August. Both are characteristic of the heath.

The chalk escarpment is tilted so steeply that the dip slope is almost as steep as the scarp slope. This is the finest ridge walk in Dorset. There are views across Swanage Bay to Peveril Point on the right and views of the heath and Poole Harbour on the left — an agreeable

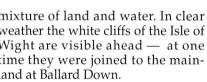

marble, which was transported from Corfe Castle in the Purbeck Hills to Poole Harbour. The marble was then carried by sea to cathedrals all over the country. The Purbeck Marblers' Road can still be traced.

On leaving Studland, the route passes through an attractive birch wood and crosses a little stream where hard ferns grow at the water's edge. When it leaves the wood the path crosses the finest area of heathland in Dorset. Pale grey sand is exposed, and this becomes dark grey further on. Patches of gorse and bracken are interspersed

▼A man-made feature on Ballard Down is this granite obelisk, put up on the heath during the 19th century.

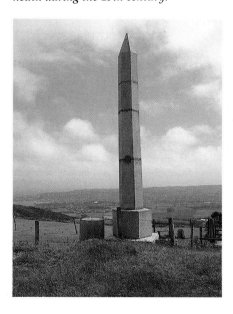

by the dominant plant, heather, with cross-leaved heath in the wetter areas. Purple moor grass also grows here and in late summer the yellow - flowerspikes of bog asphodel rise from the marshy area to the left of the path. The best time to see the heath is in the autumn, when it becomes a mixture of subtle colours.

The path leads to an enormous boulder called the Agglestone **❸**, which is 17 feet (5.1 metres) high. Boulders this size are common in mountainous areas, but in Dorset there is nothing else like it. It is also known as Devil's Anvil, or the Witchstone, and was even more impressive before it fell over onto its side in 1979. Here the sand is creamcoloured and further on the ground is littered with fragments of brown heathstone.

RIDGE WALKING

Before long, the route leaves the heath and follows the crest of the chalk escarpment of Ballard Down — a Site of Special Scientific Interest noted for its butterflies. These include the grayling, a large butterfly with a habit of aligning itself

mixture of land and water. In clear weather the white cliffs of the Isle of Wight are visible ahead — at one time they were joined to the mainland at Ballard Down.

SEA STACKS

The route passes the Ulwell Barrow and an obelisk **❸**, where an inscription says that the granite was transported from near the Mansion House in London and re-erected here in 1892. Further along the ridge two tumuli are passed on the right. Soon there is sea on both sides and Durlston Head (with Durlston Castle in silhouette) can be seen behind Peveril Point. Just before an Ordnance Survey column is reached the route crosses an ancient bank and ditch called a cross dyke.

Where the ridge reaches the sea there is spectacular coastal scenery

Wildlife of the Dorset Heath

Much of the Dorset heath has, over the years, been reclaimed for agriculture or forestry and used for the extraction of gravel. Oil has been found here as well as ball clay, which is sent to the potteries in Poole and Stoke-on-Trent; the disused clay pits make attractive small lakes.

The heath, however, remains an important site for natural history lovers. Among the more interesting plants to be found are bog myrtle (also called sweet gale on account of its delightful scent), cotton grass, heath spotted orchid, marsh gentian and royal fern. Sphagnum moss grows in the bogs, along with jointed rushes and sundew. The less acid bogs are dominated by black bog-rushes, which may be identified by the black tufts growing just above their stems.

All six British reptiles occur on the heath — adder, grass snake, smooth snake, slow-worm, common lizard and sand lizard. Roe deer are often encountered, especially in the early morning or evening; sika deer are found in the forestry plantations.

The bird for which the heath is most famous is the elusive Dartford warbler, but a much more common bird is the stonechat, which is frequently seen perching on gorse bushes. As dusk falls on the heath in summer, the churring of a nightjar can usually be heard, the pitch of its note changing slightly whenever the bird turns its head.

Dragonflies, including the blue emperor dragonfly, can be seen wherever there is water. Entomologists come to look for the heath grasshopper, the large marsh grasshopper and the bog bush-cricket, but these are likely to be missed by the less observant visitor. The tiger beetle, which is green with yellow spots, is much more common.

The Dorset heathland: home to a variety of wildlife and referred to by Thomas Hardy in several of his novels.

▲*In contrast to the open heathland, some of the path to the Agglestone is sheltered by deciduous greenery.*

coves beyond Handfast Point. Here the rock is still chalk, but instead of dropping sheer into the sea, the cliffs are broken up by grassy ledges and the chalk is stained brown. Before returning to Studland, the route passes by the edge of Studland Wood ❺ where the dark green, sharp-pointed leaves of the butcher's broom grow. Before reaching the road the track passes close enough to Studland Manor for a good view of the house and its grounds.

with glistening white cliffs and three stacks one behind the other — the Pinnacle, the Haystack and Old Harry ❹. Cormorants are common and the clifftop is bedecked in a multitude of wild flowers in the spring. Wild cabbages also grow on the clifftop.

As Handfast Point is approached the coastline becomes divided into small coves by narrow promontories. The third promontory is pierced by an arch. Between Handfast Point and Old Harry is the island called No Man's Land, which was joined to the mainland as recently as 1920. There are more promontories and

▶*Ballard Down, designated a Site of Special Scientific Interest, is owned by the National Trust.*

DORSET

Across the Dorset Downs overlooking the English Channel

A magnificent viewpoint over the western approaches to the English Channel from Black Down is the outstanding feature of this walk. The route also includes two long ridge walks along some of the highest of Dorset's seaward downlands with more splendid views. It starts from Portesham village, the boyhood home of Sir Thomas Masterman Hardy, captain of Nelson's flagship *HMS Victory*, who eventually became a vice admiral. The route climbs to a monument erected in his memory.

Much of the walk is through an area of Special Scientific Interest, particularly rich in plant and bird

FACT FILE

☀ Portesham, about 8 miles (12.8 km) south-west of Dorchester

os OLM 15, grid reference SY 603858

miles 0 1 2 3 4 5 6 7 8 9 10 miles
kms 0 1 2 3 4 5 6 7 8 9 10 11 12 13 14 15 kms

◔ 3½ hours

◖ Hilly, with two steep climbs. Wear strong shoes with a good grip or boots

P The King's Arms in Portesham allows walkers to use one of its car parks

T Buses from Weymouth

⊞ The King's Arms pub has a garden and children's play area. Other facilities in Portesham

▲Rolling countryside and the English Channel can be viewed from the hilltops. The green hairstreak butterfly (inset) is difficult to detect on a plant.

life. Evidence of early man dating from Neolithic times can be seen on the hillsides.

Portesham Ⓐ is a pleasant village tucked in a hollow among the steep Dorset downs with a clear stream overhung with ferns running beside its main street. Most of the houses are built of local stone. There is no view of the sea from here, but in a south-westerly gale you can hear the roar of the breakers on Chesil Beach, 3 miles (4.8 km) to the south.

THE WALK

PORTESHAM

The walk begins at the King's Arms in Portesham A. Approaching Portesham from the B3157 from Weymouth, turn right for the pub car parks, just before reaching Portesham village.

1 From the car park, turn left to the B3157. Turn right, then right again to walk up the village. On the left, behind the sign for Goose Hill, is Portesham House **B**, the boyhood home of Sir Thomas Masterman Hardy. Pass the church on your left and follow the road round to the right. A short distance further on turn right following the bridleway sign to the Hardy Monument **E**. Follow the lane through a gate.

2 From the gate walk straight ahead up the down, with a stone wall and double hedgerow on your left.

3 Walk to the top of the hill, ignoring the first gateway on your left. At the top of the left-hand corner of the field are two parallel stone walls. Follow the right-hand wall, and pass through two gates. The second gate leads to a farm track which, if you bear left down the hill, will lead to a barn on the left and a walled area on the right.

4 Do not follow the signpost here pointing straight ahead for the coast path, but turn left for a short way to proceed to the Hardy Monument. For a close view of the Hell Stone **C**, follow the sign straight ahead for a short distance up the down. Return to follow the sign for the Hardy Monument, bear left at the first junction, then follow the sign for the monument at the next junction. On leaving the wood **D** you will find the monument

---

The church has many interesting features including a Norman font, a beautiful 15th-century screen and a Jacobean pulpit. During the Civil War, fierce fighting took place in this area and several musket balls have been removed from the south door, which dates from the 15th century and retains its original lock and key. Portesham House **B** was Thomas Masterman Hardy's boyhood home. It is a simple, two-storey stone-built house with a stone slab roof.

Dating back to Neolithic times, to about 3,000 BC, the Hell Stone **C** is a chambered long barrow, or burial chamber. (Hel, in Northern mythology, was the Goddess of the Dead.) The nine upright stones supporting a large single flat rock were restored in 1866, possibly incorrectly, but there are traces of a barrow mound at least 88 feet (26.4 metres) long and 40 feet (12 metres) wide, with a maximum height of 5 feet (1.5 metres) associated with the stones. Frederick Treves, a Dorset historian, writes that the door opens towards the sea and the sun at its height, and that for many years the tomb was a welcome shelter for shepherds.

BLUEBELL CARPET

The woods **D**, with their pollarded oaks, beech and hazels, together with the downlands above, have been designated a Site of Special Scientific Interest. Beneath the trees many kinds of wild flowers flourish — the bluebells form a brilliant scented carpet in May. Roe deer can

◀ *The Hell Stone burial chamber dates back to Neolithic times; the tomb was restored in the 19th century.*

ALL PHOTOS BOB GIBBONS

directly in front of you on a mound. You are on Black Down **F**. There is a viewpoint **G** nearby.

▶**5** Descend to the minor road just north of the monument and turn right to follow it downhill. Ignore the first footpath sign on your right, but turn right down the second, following the sign for Corton Hill and Osmington Mills (the inland route of the Dorset Coast Path). Follow the ridge of Bronkham Hill, the whole distance pimpled with tumuli **H**. Keep straight on along the ridge through two gates, past a fingerpost on your right. Go through the next gate and again ignore a footpath sign on your right. As you approach the next gate you will see a line of electricity pylons about 100 yards (90 metres) ahead.

▶**6** Navigate carefully here. Leave the wide track just before the gate and turn right to follow a tiny path through bushes. There is a stile on your left and a signpost reading 'Corton Hill and Coryate'. (If you go through the gate and look back you will see the stile and post clearly a little to the left of the track). Follow the sign downhill with the hedge on your right.

▶**7** At the bottom of the field, turn right to cross two stiles. There is a track a short distance further on, leading left. This corner can be very muddy. Follow the track as it drops down a cleft in the hills to meet a minor road to Portesham. Turn right along the road, then right again for Little Waddon and Portesham.

Almost immediately you will see a gate on your right. Leave the road and go through the gate.

▶**8** The return route to Portesham is along the top of the ridge directly ahead that runs parallel with the minor road. The right of way differs slightly from the map at this point, and at first there is no clearly defined path. From the gate, climb to the top of the ridge bearing a little left. (There is a small concrete tank on the top.) Now follow the ridge, leaving the tank on your right, west, in the direction of Portesham. Cross two stiles and keep straight on along the ridge with a wall on your right.

▶**9** Do not go through the main gate here but bear right through a small gate beside it. Follow a farm track for a few minutes, then leave the farm track (do not go through the gate ahead) and bear left to continue along the top of the down with a post and wire fence on your right. When you see two gates ahead, go through the left hand one. Keep straight on with a stone wall on your right. In the valley on your left you will see part of Waddon Manor **J**. Climb over the next wooden pole stile and keep on towards the stone wall on your right. Go through the gate.

▶**10** Turn left down the narrow lane which brings you to the minor road to Portesham and turn right to follow the road the short distance to the village, past the King's Arms to the junction with the B3157. Turn left, then left again to the car park.

be seen among the trees. The downs form the western extremity of the acid Bagshot Beds and are studded with heathland plants, including ling and bell heather, wavy hair grass, bristle bent, wood sage, broad buckler ferns, mosses and lichens. Butterflies include the silver studded blue and the green hairstreak. Apart from birds of prey – buzzards and hawks – stonechats, scolding from the tops of gorse bushes, goldcrests and linnets may be seen.

The monument **E** to Admiral

Hardy has been compared to a factory chimney or a telephone receiver placed on end. A plaque reveals that it was erected by public subscription in 1844. However, there are wide views from this hilltop over the Channel and it seems appropriate that a great sailor should be remembered here. The novelist Thomas Hardy (who claimed the Admiral as an ancestor) could see the memorial from his bedroom window in the cottage where he was born at Higher Bockhampton. He featured

the Admiral in his only historical novel *The Trumpet Major*.

Black Down **F** is one of the original beacon hills that were used across the country as an early warning system — a great fire was lit here in 1588 to herald the approach of the Spanish Armada. During the threat of invasion by Napoleon, the 'beacon keepers' lived in a small hut beside their beacon waiting to light it, should danger threaten. A modern beacon was placed here in 1988.

The view **G** from Black Down,

▶*The grey stone church of St Peter's in Portesham village stands close by Admiral Hardy's boyhood home. The return route to Portesham is along the top of a ridge and affords a view looking east across Corton Hill (above left).*

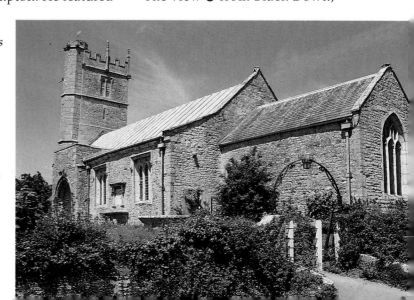

ALL PHOTOS BOB GIBBONS

over 700 feet (210 metres) above sea level, is spectacular. It commands the whole of the western approaches from Start Point in the west to Weymouth in the east. Long waves of rolling downs stretch on either side. The route, which follows one of these (Bronkham Hill), reveals more splendid views with here and there a glimpse of the Fleet — the narrow inland sea trapped behind the Chesil Bank. Bronze and Iron

◀ *The pond at Portesham. The village is at the foot of one of Dorset's oldest beacon hills, Black Down.*

Nature Walk

LYNCHETS, or hillside terraces, were produced by the first farmers who ploughed the downland hillsides to use them for arable land.

DEWPONDS, clay ponds lined with straw to hold rain water, were used by shepherds to water their flocks. They still exist on the downs.

A Stalwart Sailor

Sir Thomas Masterman Hardy, captain of Nelson's flagship *HMS Victory*, is remembered for his presence beside his dying commander at the Battle of Trafalgar in 1805. He was made a baronet in the same year.

Hardy was a fine sailor, fascinated by the sea from an early age. He was born at Kingston Russell House in 1769 and brought to live in Portesham when he was nine. At the age of 12 he went to sea as a 'captain's servant' under Captain Francis Roberts. All his life he retained his fondness for Portesham, which he called in local dialect 'Possum', and for all things made in

Dorset – mutton, cheese and above all, beer. Apparently he became very anxious if consignments of Dorset beer were late arriving on board!

'Dear Hardy', as Nelson called him, died in 1839 and the monument was erected in his memory five years later. It was built on land belonging to the Hardy family. It seems fitting that his memorial should be on this hilltop where he may often have sat as a boy, looking over the English Channel he was to fight so hard to defend.

In Daniel Maclise's painting, The Death of Nelson, *which hangs in the House of Lords, Hardy tends to the dying admiral.*

Age men buried their dead in great numbers along the length of Bronkham Hill ⑪. The seaward ridge may have been of special significance to them.

Towards the end of the walk, there are remnants of a Tudor Manor ⑫, set among gardens.

▼ *The Hardy Monument on Black Down is not renowned for its beauty. The column can be seen from far afield.*

AROUND OSMINGTON

31

PETER BAKER/PHOTOBANK INTERNATIONAL. INSET: PAUL STERRY/NATURE PHOTOGRAPHERS LTD

Along the Dorset Coast Path to an old smugglers' haunt

Chalk cliffs leading down to secluded bays make this part of the Dorset coastline particularly attractive. Inland, there are small villages to explore and the Dorset Coast Path gives walkers excellent views in good weather. The high spot of the walk undoubtedly occurs just past Osmington Mills **B**, when the path suddenly bursts upon the cliff top and there is a view over a great expanse of sea to Weymouth.

The route covers an area northeast of Weymouth, where the scenery is very diverse due to differences in the underlying rocks. These change from Purbeck stone to Kimmeridge clay, to Corallian limestone then to chalk. The rocks of the

FACT FILE

* Osmington, 5 miles (8 km) south-east of Dorchester

* Pathfinder 1332 (SY 68/78), grid reference SY 724830

miles 0   1   2   3   4   5   6   7   8   9   10 miles
kms 0   1   2   3   4   5   6   7   8   9   10   11   12   13   14   15 kms

* Allow 3 hours

* Wet grass may be encountered near the start of the walk. Muddy at Lower Dairy Farm after wet weather

P In Osmington

T Bus service from Weymouth

The Sunray at Osmington. Tearoom overlooking the sea and the Smugglers' Inn at Osmington Mills

WC At Osmington Mills

▲*Smugglers' Inn at Osmington Mills is a reminder of the illegal dealings that once took place here. The Mother Shipton moth (inset) flies during the day.*

heathland area, the Bagshot Beds, are never far away.

Osmington **A** is a village of thatched stone cottages and stone garden walls. The cottages are adorned with flowers and valerian grows outwards from the walls. One of the cottages has a thatched roof embellished with crescent-shaped decorations called scallops.

Adjoining the churchyard are the ruins of the 17th-century manor house, where steps lead down to a very old door with long iron hinges.

THE WALK

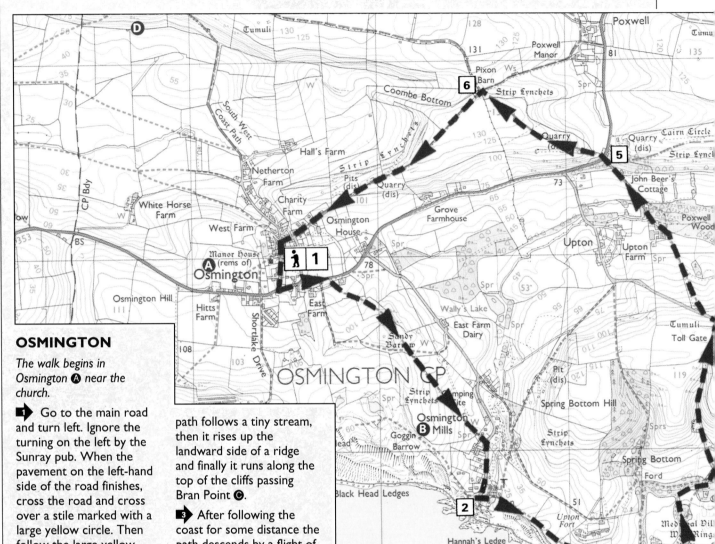

OSMINGTON

The walk begins in Osmington Ⓐ near the church.

1 Go to the main road and turn left. Ignore the turning on the left by the Sunray pub. When the pavement on the left-hand side of the road finishes, cross the road and cross over a stile marked with a large yellow circle. Then follow the large yellow circles and walk diagonally across two fields. Follow the path across the third field and continue in the same direction along the right-hand side of a hedge until you come to a stile. Go over the stile and continue along a shady path. When you come to a road, turn right to the seaside hamlet of Osmington Mills Ⓑ.

2 At the end of the road turn left at the signpost. Cross Upton Brook (which is crossed here by no fewer than six wooden bridges), turn left at the entrance to Smugglers' Inn, then turn right along the side of the inn. At first the

path follows a tiny stream, then it rises up the landward side of a ridge and finally it runs along the top of the cliffs passing Bran Point Ⓒ.

3 After following the coast for some distance the path descends by a flight of wooden steps to a stream, which is crossed by a plank bridge. Turn left and follow the stream through a wood until you come to a concrete bridge. Go over the bridge and ascend the left bank of a smaller stream. The path bends right over the tributary and continues through the wood. When you come to a lane go straight on. The lane bends right and then left and comes to a junction. Bear right here, and keep straight on until you come to a road.

4 Turn left and follow the road up a little valley to a T-junction. Turn left again and after about 70 yards

(63 metres) go through a farm gate on the right, down a track towards some farm buildings. Keep to the track and onto a road which leads up a gentle slope to the main road, the A353.

5 Cross the main road with care, go through a farm gate and up a track on the right-hand side of a small valley. When the track fades, aim for a solitary hawthorn bush leaning to the right and continue in the same direction until the grey

slate roof of Pixon Barn comes into view.

6 At the unmetalled road, bear left through two gates (one before and one after Pixon Barn). The Osmington White Horse Ⓓ is to your right. Keep going in the same direction, following first a fence and then a stone wall. Continue through a farm gate and down a shady track to a road in the village of Osmington. Go straight ahead for 80 yards (72 metres), then turn left to return to the start.

▶ *While staying in Osmington in 1861, Constable painted Weymouth Bay. The painting hangs in the National Gallery.*

NATIONAL GALLERY, LONDON

Nature Walk

THE NIGHTJAR winters in Africa, but flies to Britain towards the end of April. It seeks out lowland heath and chalk downland, typical of the landscape surrounding Osmington.

THE NIGHTJAR is difficult to spot as it is most active at night and is well camouflaged by its colouring. In flight, white tail and wing patches show as it swoops while hunting its insect prey.

THE BIRD has a huge mouth. If other birds attempt to invade the nest, it threatens them by hissing. It scoops up insects with its wide gape, which is surrounded by bristles.

CHRIS ROSE

In 1816, the artist John Constable spent his honeymoon in the village. He produced two paintings of the area, one entitled *Osmington Village* and the other *Weymouth Bay*.

From Osmington Mills the route follows part of the Dorset Coast Path, which takes to the hills here to avoid the built-up area around Weymouth. From this height there is a beautiful view to the left looking along a valley to Holworth. The Osmington White Horse ❶ can be clearly seen from here. This is the only white horse chalk figure that has a rider — King George III, who was a regular visitor to this part of the country. There is a view of the Osmington White Horse towards the end of the walk, just past Pixon Barn. From here it is possible to see the chalk figure on the right of the chalk escarpment.

CLIFF-TOP INN

The Smugglers' Inn at Osmington Mills is described on the signboard as a 13th-century smugglers' haunt, but the present building is not as old as this. There used to be a cliff-top path to the west from here, but from the far end of the car park it is clear how this path has now completely disappeared as a result of erosion by the sea. This evidence of erosion makes it possible to imagine Britain becoming separated from France

▶ *A section of the walk follows the Dorset Coast Path. The headland of White Nothe can be seen to the east.*

and the Isle of Wight from the mainland, over thousands of years.

Before long the path passes through a thicket; when it emerges the headland of White Nothe comes into view ahead, with St Adhelm's Head to the right of it. In the novel *Moonfleet* by J Meade Falkner, John Trenchard was carried up the cliff path to White Nothe by Elzevir Block. Along the shore there is a wreck of an old ship whose bare ribs are a favourite perch for cormorants. At Bran Point ❸ there is a series of ledges of Corallian limestone which dip away to the east.

WOODLAND GREENERY

The path passes a meadow where bird's-foot trefoil grows, then it descends into a little valley. Here the route turns into a wood, where hart's tongue fern and pendulous sedge flourish. Hart's tongue does not look like a fern as its leaves are not divided up into pinnae (feathery

PETER BAKER/PHOTOBANK INTERNATIONAL

fronds). However, you can identify it as a fern by the fruiting bodies on the back of the leaves. Pendulous sedge may be recognized as a sedge by its triangular stems.

CHALK QUARRY

On leaving the wood, the route follows a lane through lush meadows backed by woodland. Another stretch of woodland comes later on the route, but the vegetation is not as luxuriant here as it is in the valley.

A wide variety of wild flowers grows in the valley, but pride of place must go to the nodding thistles with their big, round purple flower-heads. On the left is a quarry where the chalk may be seen dipping to the north. The chalk was formed over a period of 30 million years from the skeletons of tiny animals called diatoms that accumulated on the floor of the sea.

Along the right-hand side of the valley there are traces of ancient cultivation terraces called strip lynchets. Both sides of the valley are covered in gorse bushes, which attract stonechats.

From the top of the hill, a Bronze Age burial mound (or tumulus) can be seen in a field on the left. There are 1,800 of these tumuli in Dorset.

LARK SONG

The final section of the walk passes Pixon Barn, which is an isolated stone building with a slate roof and walled farmyard. Rabbits are common in this area, and larks may be heard singing overhead. As the route descends, it runs along the crest of a ridge with views on both sides. On the left, the Isle of Portland is linked to the mainland

The Smugglers' Route

Between about 1750 and 1840 vast quantities of smuggled brandy, tea, silk and tobacco were brought ashore on the south coast of England and distributed inland by wagon or packhorse. One of the regular landing places was Osmington Mills and from 1790 until 1800 what is now Smugglers' Inn was the headquarters of the smuggler-chief Pierre la Tour, who was known in England as French Peter. He eventually married the landlord's daughter, Arabella Carless, and took her back to France with him, where they lived comfortably on his illicit fortune. It was not until much later that the inn acquired its present name.

The smugglers' route from Osmington Mills to Sherborne passed the cottage at Lower Bockhampton where Thomas Hardy was born in 1840. Smuggling had ceased by Hardy's time, but it obviously caught the boy's imagination. He remembered his grandfather telling him how he had hidden kegs of smuggled spirit in the cottage and cut a window in the side of the porch to look out for Revenue Officers. The cottage was ideally situated as a staging post as it was on the edge of the heath.

Wreckers tried to cause shipwrecks deliberately, to profit from the cargo.

The route used by the smugglers, called Snail Creep, can still be seen to this day running north and south from the cottage.

by no more than a narrow strip of shingle; on the right is a valley of Kimmeridge clay and you can see the village of Sutton Poyntz. The white horse is also visible, but it appears to be foreshortened because of the angle. Finally, the route follows a lane shaded by sycamore trees, which leads back into Osmington. A giant ammonite can be seen in a house wall — a common sight in this fossiliferous county.

▶ *The Osmington White Horse was produced, like other hill figures, by cutting the turf away from a chalk hillside. If not regularly weeded, vegetation grows back, obscuring the figure. The roofs of Poxwell Manor (above left) in Poxwell village.*

HARDY'S HOME

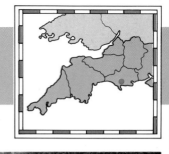

32

A varied walk through water-meadows, woods, fields and heathland

▲*Hardy's Cottage is set off by a colourful cottage garden. Hobbies (inset) are summertime falcons on the heaths.*

This area is rich in its associations with Thomas Hardy. The author grew up around here and the countryside was the setting for many incidents in his novels.

Hardy's Cottage Ⓐ is where Thomas Hardy was born and where he lived until he was a young man. It was built in 1800 by John Hardy, the writer's great-grandfather, and is now owned by the National Trust.

Hardy wrote *Under the Greenwood Tree* and *Far from the Madding Crowd* in this idyllic setting.

In Hardy's imagination, the fictional 'Egdon Heath' stretched from Dorchester to Bournemouth. The heath features in many of his poems and novels, notably *The Return of the Native*, which uses the wild

▼*The bridleway on the route towards Troy Town Farm passes through peaceful, hedge-lined fields.*

FACT FILE

✳ Higher Bockhampton, 4 miles (6.4 km) east of Dorchester, off the A35

OS OLM 15, grid reference SY 725921

miles 0	1	2	3	4	5	6	7	8	9	10 miles
kms 0	1 2	3	4	5	6	7	8	9 10	11 12	13 14 15 kms

◔ Allow 6 hours or 3 hours

◗ Some inclines. Walking shoes recommended. **Warning:** walk crosses fast dual carriageway

P National Trust car park at Hardy's Cottage

T Bus services from Dorchester, Bournemouth and Blandford

🍺 The Prince of Wales and the Blue Vinney in Puddletown, 🍴 3 miles (4.8 km) from start

WC 1 mile (1.6 km) from the start in a layby on the A35

🏰 Hardy's Cottage is a National Trust property. The exterior can be viewed from April to the end October, from 11am to 6pm. Admission to the interior by appointment only

THE WALK

HIGHER BOCKHAMPTON

To reach the start of the walk, follow the signs from the A35 to Higher Bockhampton and then to Hardy's Cottage Ⓐ.

1 From the car park, follow the signpost labelled 'Hardy's Cottage via Woodland Path'. The path takes you through mature woodland, containing plane, beech, oak and some rhododendron.

2 Leave Hardy's Cottage and return to his monument

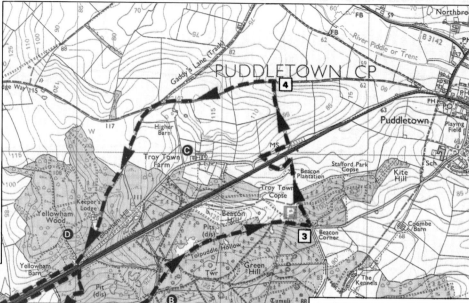

High on your left is a mature conifer plantation on the top of Beacon Hill. You are now walking through Tolpuddle Hollow.

3 At Beacon Corner, turn sharp left to walk up beside Beacon Plantation. Shortly a car park is signposted. Go straight ahead to the crest of the hill then down the track that slopes away from you between hazel trees. When you reach the new A35 dual carriageway, go left through the underpass then right along the old A35 and left again up the bridleway heading north. At the brow of the hill there are good views of Dorset farmland to your right.

4 At the T-junction of bridleways, turn left to walk along level ground through hazel hedges on both sides. As you pass Higher Barn on your left you have a good view of

Troy Town Farm Ⓒ. Shortly after Higher Barn, go through a metal-barred gate then go immediately left through the next metal gate on your left, following the blue waymark. It is important to make sure you do go immediately left or you will find yourself walking along the Ridge Way. In 50 yards (45 metres) there is a large mature oak tree on your left, followed shortly by another. The grassy track rises towards Yellowham Wood Ⓓ, with a hedge of hazel and oak trees to your left. Yellowham Wood contains oak, beech, blackthorn and chestnut. The path through the wood slopes down quite steeply. The thatched Keeper's Lodge is to your right. The grassy path joins a well used track that descends to the A35. Turn right at the old A35 and walk down the road for 500 yards (450 metres), then — taking great care — over the new dual carriageway at the signpost for the Bockhamptons.

5 Turn sharp left along the new footpath and

to follow the blue waymark in a north-easterly direction. The sandy path rises gently through coniferous trees. You soon come to a junction of five forest tracks. Go straight across, continuing in a north-easterly direction. The path curves gently to the right on a slight incline. The woods are now more

open and of a deciduous nature. Eventually the sandy path gives way to a stonier track through much younger deciduous and conifer woodland (part of 'Egdon Heath' Ⓑ). At a junction with an extremely well-defined, chalky track, go straight across, now walking in an easterly direction down the hill.

◄*After passing Lane House and a hay barn, fine vistas of Dorset farmland stretch ahead. Kingston Maurward House (below) is now home to the Dorset College of Agriculture.*

heathland as a setting for many of its dramatic incidents. Bhompston, Duddle and Puddletown Heaths **B**, the inspiration for 'Egdon Heath', are now managed mainly by the Forestry Commission. Troy Town **C** is the town of 'Roy' in *Far from the Madding Crowd*, but unfortunately the Bucks Head Inn, the place where Joseph Poorgrass stopped with the body of Fanny Robin, has now been demolished.

A little further along the walk is Yellowham Wood **D**, the 'Yalbury Wood' of *Under the Greenwood Tree*. Keeper's Lodge there is the model for the home of Fancy Day. According to local superstition, the wood was the haunt of 'The Wild Man o' Yall'm', who reputedly fathered many illegitimate offspring in the neighbouring area.

WESSEX LANDSCAPE

'Mellstock', which was frequently introduced in Hardy's novels and poems and is especially associated with *Under the Greenwood Tree*, was Hardy's fictitious name for an amalgam of three Dorset villages — Higher Bockhampton **E**, Lower Bockhampton and Stinsford.

Soon the route leads you to Kingston Maurward **F**, the 'Knapwater House' of *Desperate Remedies*. The house stands in a

---

continue until you are directly opposite your exit from Yellowham Wood. Turn right up the footpath back to Hardy's Monument, where you start the second half of this figure-of-eight walk through Higher Bockhampton **E**. Walk back to the road. Turn left and left again at the top of the short rise. In 50 yards (45 metres) go right along a well-defined chalk track, with Lane House on your left. As you come to a hay barn, go left through a metal-barred gate and immediately right along the edge of the field, keeping the hedge and the barn to your right. Walk down across the field and at its corner go through a metal-barred gate, then straight ahead across the field in front of you. At this point the footpath is not well defined, but is clear once you are on it. Continue until you reach a farm track and the road.

6 Walk straight across the road through a squeeze-stile by the side of a metal-barred gate, following the blue waymarked bridleway sign. The track is clearly marked across the field and there is a barbed wire fence on your right. Head towards the next metal-barred gate. Go through this and continue along the track. There are sycamore trees on your left and Kingston Maurward Park **F** is on your right. Go through a five-bar gate adjacent to a sycamore tree. Continue to the next gate and through it onto a road, then between a group of buildings to a junction. Turn right and follow the metalled road around, with Kingston Maurward House high on your left, to a T-junction. Go left and left again, taking the road to the church of St Michael in Stinsford **G**.

7 On leaving the church, turn right and walk down a metalled path, then a gravel path down to a stream. Cross the stream and turn left. Go straight across a junction with another footpath. Continue on the gravel path with streams on either side — this is the the Frome Valley **H**.

8 When you come to the road turn left and cross the bridge heading for Lower Bockhampton. Turn right immediately after a thatched cottage. Walk down to Kingston Dairy House, through the farmyard then through a metal gate on the opposite side. Turn right through another metal-barred gate into a field. Head for the house on the skyline. The River Frome is at the bottom of the field on your right. Cross a step-stile marked with a yellow arrow and follow the clearly defined path. Continue alongside the hedge on your right until the path veers left and away from the hedge to the left-hand side of the house you have been aiming for. Go through a metal-barred gate and turn left up the gravel track.

9 On reaching a road go straight across, up the track towards Pine Lodge Farm. Walk to a metal-barred gate, go through it and straight on with the hedge on your left. As you walk along the edge of a field, Duddle Heath, Heedless William's Pond **J** and Rainbarrows **K** are to your right.

10 At the corner of the field, go through a wood and metal gate out onto a track in a wooded area. Turn left and walk down the hill. Where the path forks, take the right-hand fork to a junction and go left through the wood. At the bottom of the hill there is a clearing with some picnic benches. Go right and follow the track back to the car park.

magnificently timbered park and is now the home of the Dorset College of Agriculture. The park is impeccably maintained, with many conservation areas. The beautiful grounds and gardens are a tribute to the care and dedication of the college staff and students.

Further on is Stinsford **G**, one of the models for 'Mellstock'. The church of St Michael, with which Hardy was associated throughout his life, is found in the village.

Thomas Hardy (1840-1928)

KOBAL COLLECTION

The famous novelist was born in Higher Bockhampton, a hamlet in the heart of the Dorset countryside. As a boy he roamed the fields and woods near his home and attended the village school, where he studied Latin, German and French and read the novels of Sir Walter Scott and Alexandre Dumas, before finishing his formal education in Dorchester. During this time he was fully involved in the country community and attended the church of St Michael in Stinsford. He also played the fiddle at weddings and dances.

As a young man, Hardy worked in London as an assistant architect. His self-education included extensive reading of the works of Shelley, Browning, Dickens, Swinburne and others. He wrote his first article and had many of his poems rejected by periodicals.

He married Emma Lavinia Gifford in 1874 and soon after paid for the publication of his first novel, *Desperate Remedies*. This was followed in quick succession by

Tess, director Roman Polanski's 1979 film of Hardy's famous 'Wessex' novel, starring Nastassja Kinski, was actually shot in Brittany.

Under the Greenwood Tree and *A Pair of Blue Eyes*. *Far from the Madding Crowd* was serialized in the *Cornhill Magazine*.

Hardy was a true countryman, chronicling the impact of urban culture on the traditional way of life of country people. He wrote with an intimate knowledge of the natural world, of farming and of the country community itself. Hardy was a regional novelist, and part of his enduring fascination is his imagined county of Wessex. He mixed his fictional people and places with those that existed at the time. Today, it is still possible to visit those places and breathe the very stuff of the novels. He is as popular in modern times as he was in his own lifetime, though, contrary to what he would have wished, it is for his novels rather than his poems that he is most remembered.

▲*Between Stinsford and Lower Bockhampton, the path has streams overhung by trees on both sides.*

'The Valley of the Great Dairies', so vividly described in *Tess of the D'Urbervilles*, is, in reality, the Frome Valley **H**. Here you will find verdant pastures and huge herds of cows in a valley 'in which milk and butter grew to rankness'. It was near Bockhampton Bridge that Hardy had Angel Clare carry four dairy-maids through the water covering the road, as they were on their way to a service at 'Mellstock'.

SCENES FROM FICTION

As you return towards the start of the walk you pass Heedless William's Pond **J**. Hardy used the pond's real name in *The Fiddler of the Reels*, where he describes how a careless carter drove his vehicle into the pond and was drowned. Hardy used the tumuli known as Rainbarrows **K** as the centre of his 'Egdon Heath', although they are actually on the western fringe. This spot is featured in *The Return of the Native* and *The Dynasts*.

PHOTOS TOP & BOTTOM PETER BAKER/PHOTOBANK INTERNATIONAL

▲*The water-meadows bordering the River Frome provide rich grazing. The river is popular with trout fishermen.*

33

DORSET

◄*Once the scene of a tragic shipping disaster, the undercut cliffs in the bay between Winspit and Seacombe offer breathtaking sea views. The rare early spider orchid (inset) can sometimes be seen on the clifftops. Worth Matravers (below) is famous for its Purbeck stone.*

ANDREW TAYLOR. INSET: ROBIN FLETCHER/SWIFT PICTURE LIBRARY

FACT FILE

✳ Worth Matravers, off the B3069, 3½ miles (5.6km) west of Swanage

⊙S Outdoor Leisure Map 15, grid reference SY 974776

miles 0 1 2 3 4 5 6 7 8 9 10 miles
kms 0 1 2 3 4 5 6 7 8 9 10 11 12 13 14 15 kms

◔ Allow 3 hours

◼ One steep ascent and some stony paths. Take windproof clothing. The clifftop path is mainly unfenced and the quarry galleries and caves are unsafe to enter; not suitable for small children

P Large public car park at the start

🍴 Square and Compass pub and tea rooms in Worth Matravers

WC At car park

A breathtaking coastal walk through the Purbeck quarries

With magnificent views throughout its length, this walk takes in some of the most spectacular coastal scenery in southern England. Worth Matravers lies in a sheltered position, about a mile (1.6km) from the sea.

Today, it is a tranquil village of charming stone cottages, but Worth has a long and interesting history. Called 'Wrde' in the Domesday Book, the village was clearly well established in Norman times. The name Matravers results from this land being owned by the Matravaux family until the 14th century.

There is further evidence of medieval occupation in the nearby strip lynchets, remains of terraced fields cultivated in those days, on the hillsides above Winspit Bottom Ⓐ. Worth Matravers was chiefly known, however, as the centre of the Purbeck stone-quarrying industry.

MANY DIFFERENT FLOWERS

The stony path from Worth to Winspit is notable for the great variety of flowers along the verges. Dog rose, vetches, field scabious and

DEREK FORSS

THE WALK

WORTH MATRAVERS – DANCING LEDGE

The walk begins from the well signposted public car park on the way into Worth Matravers.

1 Leaving the car park, turn right and go downhill on the road. Bear right at the junction beside the pub and continue downhill through the village. At Squint Cottage, bear left past the village green and duck pond, then after 20 paces take the second left into a no-through road. At the end of a terrace of stone cottages, cross the stile to your left and follow a well-defined track, descending via a series of stiles through Winspit Bottom **Ⓐ**, before emerging on the low headland above the sea.

2 After detouring to your right to inspect the main Winspit Quarry workings **Ⓑ**, bear left and follow the track towards a smaller quarry. The path winds steeply, via an uneven flight of steps,

around the head of this quarry. The clifftop path takes you to the south of the tiny cove, then turns eastward along the coast, crossing two stiles at either side of a small open-cast

quarry **Ⓒ**. The track now curves gently inland to head between some scrubby hawthorn bushes. About 30 paces past a pile of quarried blocks, an almost-hidden stile on the

right leads downhill via a flight of steps into Seacombe Bottom.

3 At the bottom of the steps, turn right. The path leads to an area of open ground where a waymark

rosebay willowherb mingle with coastal species, such as sea bindweed, bugloss and red valerian. Honeysuckle and old-man's beard climb up the shrubs of elder, blackthorn and hawthorn.

Now disused, Winspit **Ⓑ** is the oldest of the local quarry works. It was also the most productive, and was worked until the early 1950s. Stone was taken both from the cliff face and from the broad 'galleries' going deep underground. Quarried stone blocks were lowered up to 30

feet (9m) from the man-made plateau above the cliff face, into flat-bottomed barges waiting below. Two smaller galleries, below the clifftop to the east of the bay, now provide a home for a colony of rare horseshoe bats.

SHIPWRECKED

On 6 January 1786, in violent storm conditions, the East-Indiaman *Halsewell* was driven into the bay between Winspit and Seacombe. The vessel broke up on a submerged ledge beneath the undercut cliffs, and the captain was drowned along with 187 others. In a dramatic rescue by local quarrymen, 82 survivors,

◄ *The top of Winspit Quarry still bears a few traces of the small, terraced fields cultivated in medieval times.*

ANDREW TAYLOR

stone points you left, across a plank bridge and uphill towards Seacombe Cliff. (Alternatively detour right at the marker stone to examine the quarry workings **D**). The route continues past the gun turret **E**, before veering inland to skirt around the top of two quarries; the second is Hedbury Quarry **F**, sometimes called Cannon Cove. A stile set in the fence on the right of the path gives access for a detour to the floor of the quarry, although the descent is a steep scramble on a loose surface. The main route continues, via the stile above Cannon Cove, along the cliff top to Dancing Ledge **G**.

4 Cross the stile above Dancing Ledge and turn right for a short, easy scramble down onto the ledge itself, but exercise caution. Alternatively, turn left and cross the adjacent stile, following the smugglers' track signposted to Spyway Barn car park. The path climbs steeply up a grassy hillside, before

turning into a sandy cutting that is conspicuous from below. A waymark stone stands at the top of the ascent, pointing northwards to Spyway Barn, visible ahead. The path leads through a gateway, across a meadow to stone steps set into a wall. Cross over the wall and continue through the two gates beside the cottages. The path turns briefly left around the back of the farm buildings before continuing north to cross the Priest's Way.

5 Turn left along Priest's Way and continue, via a series of stiles and gates, past an open-cast pit **H**, to Eastington Farm. Crossing a stone stile by the gate to the right of the farm, take the left-hand track, leading to a stile in the south-west corner of the field. Cross this stile, and three more, to emerge on a metalled road. Turn left, and continue to the road junction opposite the entry to Worth Museum and Craft Centre. Turn right to return to the car park.

DEREK FORSS

▲ *This ancient ammonite fossil can be easily spotted on the edge of the open-cast quarry east of Winspit. Noteworthy for its many quarried caves or galleries, the extensive Seacombe Quarry (below) once produced blocks of Purbeck stone that weighed up to 15 tons.*

Closer inspection reveals this to be a metal turret **E**, installed in 1940, where a lone machine gunner had the unenviable task of protecting this stretch of coast from potential air and seaborne attack.

SHIPPING PROBLEMS

At Hedbury Quarry **F**, stone was extracted from caves on two levels. Founded in the 18th century by the Eidbury family, from whom their name derives, the workings are accessible only via a steep track. The quarried stone had to be shipped out on barges brought alongside the treacherous cliff face below. The site

who had struggled to a rock above the waves, were hauled up the cliff face to safety. This tragic drama took place at a point almost immediately below the small open-cast quarry, or 'ridden hole' **C**, to the left of the path, ½ mile (800m) east of Winspit. On the eastern rim of the pit, a giant ammonite fossil has been exposed.

HEAVY STONE BLOCKS

At Seacombe, gaping galleries plunge deeply below ground in the largest of the cliffside quarry workings **D**. Blocks weighing up to 15 tons were hewn out from here. In places, the gallery ceilings reach a height of 13 feet (4m).

Just off the path on the east side of Seacombe Cliff stands what appears at first to be an igloo tent, pitched upon an exposed site.

ANDREW TAYLOR

▲ *At Dancing Ledge the walk descends to the sea. The tidal bathing pool here was blasted out of the rocks for the recreation of local schoolboys.*

▶ *A lone cannon from Napoleonic times faces the sea at Hedbury Quarry. To this day its exact history remains a mystery.*

of the derrick used to lower the stone blocks remains visible.

The seaward-facing cannon here is a 12-pounder of the Napoleonic period, though the circumstances of its presence on the site remain a mystery. This secluded area is home to a large colony of rabbits and flowers such as blue fleabane, viper's bugloss and wild carrot.

DANCING LEDGE

Dancing Ledge **G** is one of the few points on the walk with direct access to the tideline. The cave created by the quarrymen on the landward side of the cove now shelters a colony of bats. Thomas Pellat, headmaster of the nearby Durnford House School, had the tidal bathing pool blasted out of the solid rock in the late 19th century.

The ledge itself, a broad plateau projecting into the sea, is deeply rutted where quarried stone was carried by hand-cart to the water's edge for loading. This was a popular spot for smuggling activities because contraband cargoes could readily be hidden in the caves.

The Priest's Way is an ancient drove road, running for the most part between dry-stone walls. Its

name dates back to the Middle Ages, when the priest from the prosperous parish of Worth would trudge across country to perform services in Swanage, which was then a tiny fishing village. On a clear day there are superb views eastwards from the Priest's Way to Swanage and the Isle of Wight.

Some quarrying is still carried out in the area, and as you return to Worth, you pass a recently exposed open-cast pit **H** on your right.

Quarrying in Purbeck

Purbeck stone has long been highly prized as a building material for castles and cathedrals. The great cliff-face quarries were begun between 1700 and 1900. Prior to this, the stone was extracted via shafts sunk 50 feet (15m) or more into the ground. Lanes were driven outwards from the bottom of the shaft into the rock seam. Stone 'legs' were built to shore up the ceiling.

Until the early years of the 20th century, quarrymen worked deep underground with only a candle for illumination. They had no machinery and only donkey power to move the stone away from the working face. Accidents were frequent, and local archives record many incidents that involved the loss of life or limb.

The decline of quarrying started

with the Industrial Revolution, when cheaply produced bricks replaced stone as a building material. Loss of orders led to the closure of many quarries, and skilled men drifted into other occupations. The increasing use of concrete in the 1920s served to deepen the slump, and the industry has never recovered.

A certain amount of quarrying continues in the area, mostly producing aggregate for the construction of roads. The National Trust, however, owns several open-cast quarries near Acton that supply quality stone for restoration work.

In the early years of this century, donkeys were used to lift great blocks of stone from the face. But the growing use of concrete helped end the quarrying of Purbeck stone.

ABOVE LYME BAY

DORSET

the southern coast of England.

From the beach it is a steep climb to the cliff tops. As you climb, you skirt Cain's Folly **B**, one of many landslips that have occurred along this notoriously crumbling coastline. The reason for the landslips is the underlying geology of the region. Porous rocks are sandwiched in between tilted layers of impervious clays and shales. Rainwater collects in the porous strata and its weight causes areas to slide into the sea.

UNDERCLIFF ANIMALS

The scars left by these landslips are soon colonized by new vegetation. Because they are relatively inaccessible and useless as farmland, they make important new habitats for small mammals such as rabbits and foxes, as well as for a wide variety of birds. Finches, tits,

▼*The pebble beach at Charmouth, a Regency and Victorian town, offers good opportunities for fossil-hunting.*

A fossil beach and dramatic landslips on National Trust land

▲*The Lyme Bay coast has cliffs, slumped undercliffs caused by landslips, and beaches of sand, shingle or rock. The great green bush-cricket (inset) lives in vegetated areas of undercliff.*

This walk starts in the small seaside town of Charmouth. The rocky beach **A** here is not good for bathing but still attracts many people. They come to look for the fossil remains of ammonites and other prehistoric marine creatures, relics of the time when this area was covered by a shallow tropical sea. A small exhibition centre near the beach provides useful information.

The best time for fossil-hunting is after a storm, when the gales bring new rocks crashing down from the cliffs, but the area is so rich that fragments may be found even at the height of the summer season.

The beach, like much of the course of this walk, gives excellent views of the coastline of Lyme Bay, stretching away south-west to Lyme Regis and east to beyond the distinctive summit of the well-named Golden Cap, the highest point on

DEREK PRATT. INSET: ROBIN FLETCHER/SWIFT PICTURE

AA PICTURE LIBRARY

FACT FILE

✳ Charmouth, 1½ miles northeast of Lyme Regis

◻S Pathfinder 1316 (SY 29/39), grid reference SY 366931

miles 0 1 2 3 4 5 6 7 8 9 10 miles
kms 0 1 2 3 4 5 6 7 8 9 10 11 12 13 14 15 kms

◔ 2 hours

⬛ Good paths, with one fairly steep climb. Windproof clothing recommended

P Town or beach car parks in Charmouth

🍴 Pubs, fish and chips, and cafés in Charmouth

WC Near the car parks

I National Trust Information Centre on Stonebarrow Hill

THE WALK

CHARMOUTH – STONEBARROW HILL

The walk starts from the wooden footbridge near the beach car park in Charmouth.

1 Depending on the state of the tide, explore the beach **A** now or on your return. Cross the footbridge over the River Char and walk up a grassy slope ahead. Follow the path up to and then along the cliff edge above Cain's Folly **B**.

2 At the top of the climb is a stile. Go straight on, following a sign to Golden Cap, 2 miles (3.2km) away. The stony path descends steeply. Pass to the right of Westhay Farm, following the South West Coast Path.

3 At a signpost reading 'Seatown 3 miles', go straight ahead, through cow pastures, crossing footbridges and stiles.

4 At the top of a rise in a grassy field, where the coast path goes straight ahead to Golden Cap, take a path to the left signposted to Stonebarrow and Morecombelake. Pass to the right of Ridge Barn and follow a grassy track, with a hedge on your right. Go through a gate and follow a clear path across a field, with Upcot Farm over to your right.

5 At the edge of the field, turn left onto the track that leads from Upcot and bear left to follow a bridleway towards Stonebarrow Hill. You soon pass through another gate and emerge onto the lower slopes of Chardown Hill **C**. Near the top, cross a stile and then some open grassland towards the summit plateau.

6 At the top, turn left and walk along the ridge of Stonebarrow Hill **D** to a National Trust Information Centre, then continue to the end of a grassy area.

7 Head diagonally left through a hedge and walk across to the cliff top to regain the coastal path. Turn right, climb the stile and retrace your steps to the start of the walk.

warblers, robins and woodpeckers all breed in these coastal enclaves, while kestrels hunt for voles and lizards all along the coast.

The route continues parallel with the cliff along the South West Coast Path through rolling cow pasture cut by small streams. The whole area is part of the Golden Cap Estate, which is farmed and managed by the National Trust, which makes sure that fences, stiles, bridges and paths are well maintained.

UP THE HILL

The route leaves the coast and starts to climb steadily inland, past the well-restored Ridge Barn to the hamlet of Upcot. Another climb, the last of the walk, takes you on to Chardown Hill **C**. Here there is an opportunity for a well-earned rest as you admire the views along the coast and inland across the Dorset hills. The path then runs along the

◄ *Golden Cap, the highest point on the south coast at 627 feet (191m), is east of our route but often catches the eye.*

spine of Stonebarrow Hill **D** and leads you towards the National Trust Information Centre, which is housed in a stone building that was once a radar station.

There is a wealth of wild flowers on the open heathland. Heather and gorse bloom profusely in late summer and blackberries and butterflies are abundant. Much of this is due to the National Trust's policy of limiting the use of pesticides and herbicides on its farmland.

From the Information Centre you descend the way you came, with views of Lyme Regis and its famous stone breakwater, the Cobb, ahead of you. If you time your return well, you will see the sun setting over the sea or the hills of Devon — depending on the time of year — as you return to the beach at Charmouth.

GEORGE WRIGHT

A Hidden Gem

DORSET

MIKE WILKES/AQUILA

A historic village and a ridge-top walk on the Dorset downs

GEORGE WRIGHT

To the north of Dorchester, several chalk streams flowing southwards to meet up with the River Frome have carved deep valleys through the downs. Some of these valleys contain seldom-visited villages that are packed with interest. Perhaps the most charming of these, Sydling St Nicholas, is the focus of this circular walk.

FEROCIOUS GARGOYLES

The walk begins by the Church of St Nicholas **A** on the west side of the village. The building dates from the 15th century and is in the elaborate late Perpendicular style, with a lofty tower decorated with some ferocious gargoyles. Inside there are some fine screens and monuments from the 18th and 19th centuries.

Beside the church is a Georgian manor house, Sydling Court, which

incorporates part of a Tudor house once owned by the politician and diplomat Sir Francis Walsingham, who was principal secretary to Queen Elizabeth I from 1573 until his death in 1590.

The walk continues into the village past the base of an old stone cross, which marks the place where Sydling's annual fair has been held every December 6th since at least the Middle Ages.

Most of the cottages in the village are thatched and built of flint and Ham stone, a much-prized golden limestone quarried just over the Somerset border to the north-west. Often, the flint and stone are laid in alternate courses for decorative

▲Sydling's Waterside Lane is very attractive, with thatched stone cottages by the stream. The dabchick or little grebe (top left) swims on Sydling Water. The village's most impressive house is Sydling Court (below left).

GEORGE WRIGHT

FACT FILE

⁂ Sydling St Nicholas, 6½ miles (10.4km) north-west of Dorchester, off the A37

▭ Pathfinder 1318 (SY 69/79), grid reference SY 630993

miles 0 1 2 3 4 5 6 7 8 9 10 miles
kms 0 1 2 3 4 5 6 7 8 9 10 11 12 13 14 15 kms

◔ Allow 2½ hours

▬ Fairly hilly, with one long, gentle climb and several shorter ones. Chalk and flint paths may be hard underfoot; walking boots or shoes recommended

P In Church Lane or off-road in the village

T Infrequent buses from Dorchester, Yeovil and Sherborne, Tel. (01935) 76233 or (01823) 272033

▤ Sydling St Nicholas has a pub
⍩ and a shop

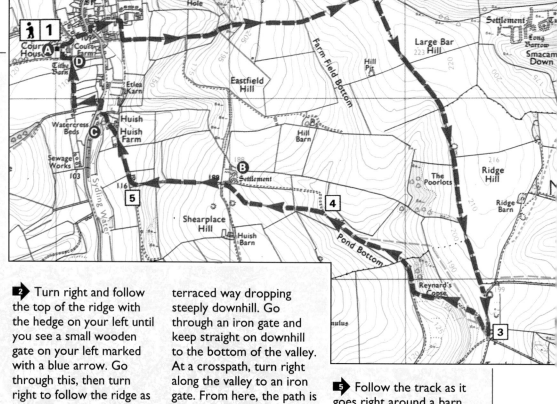

THE WALK

SYDLING ST NICHOLAS

This circular walk begins in the lane leading to Sydling St Nicholas's church Ⓐ. The village is best approached along a byroad off the A37 Dorchester to Yeovil road just north of Grimstone.

1 Walk back down the lane to the Dorchester road. Turn left and immediately right down East Street. At a T-junction, turn right. When the road bears to the right, keep straight on, following the blue arrow bridleway sign down a concrete path. Follow the track as it turns left uphill. When it turns to the right, keep straight on through a gate along a green, terraced path leading uphill to another gate. Do not go through, but continue uphill to the right of the gate to a further gate on the skyline. Go through and climb the field ahead, with a hedge on your left. Cross a field track and continue straight ahead as the path dips and climbs to a crosspath in front of a hedge.

2 Turn right and follow the top of the ridge with the hedge on your left until you see a small wooden gate on your left marked with a blue arrow. Go through this, then turn right to follow the ridge as before, with the hedge now on your right. This brings you to another wooden gate. Go through and bear a little left across the corner of the field towards the hedge running along the top. A post with two blue arrows at the hedge marks a crosspath. Bear right to follow the ridge once more.

3 Go through a wooden gate and turn very sharply right, with a fence and hedge close on your right. The path becomes a green terraced way dropping steeply downhill. Go through an iron gate and keep straight on downhill to the bottom of the valley. At a crosspath, turn right along the valley to an iron gate. From here, the path is ill-defined. Bear slightly left to a fence, then keep straight along the valley with the fence on your left. The path soon becomes clear again.

4 When the fence bends left uphill, follow the path left beside it and climb to the highest point. To the right of the path are the hollows and embankments of a Celtic Settlement Ⓑ. Follow the sunken path as it drops steeply down into the valley.

5 Follow the track as it goes right around a barn, then bears left round Huish Farm to cross Sydling Water Ⓒ. At a T-junction, turn left to meet the road from Dorchester. Turn right for about 50 yards (45m), then first left up a lane. Turn right on a crosstrack, and go through a gate and into a farmyard. Turn immediately left to walk past a huge tithe barn Ⓓ on your right. Soon after, a stile on your right leads into the churchyard and back to the lane where the walk began.

---

effect. Several brooks and rills run through the village, and the cottages are connected to the roads and to one another by footbridges.

A long, steady climb out of the village takes you up onto the downs, where you walk south along a ridge. There are wonderful views west over the Sydling Valley, and south to the seaward-facing hills.

CELTIC SETTLEMENT

You walk down a banked green track into Pond Bottom, then climb again to where there are some low banks and enclosures, the remains of a large Celtic settlement Ⓑ. In the Dark Ages, these downlands were well-populated, and several settlements are scattered along the hilltops. The outlines of their small fields or lynchets can be seen on the surrounding hillsides.

This site, on a saddle of land between two swelling hills, provides another magnificent view over the valley. The route drops down into the valley and passes Huish Farm, with its handsome, lichen-crusted, brick boundary wall, before crossing Sydling Water Ⓒ. This little chalk stream is a favourite spawning ground for salmon swimming inland from Poole. Dabchicks dart around huge stands of reeds and flags, while kingfishers and nightingales haunt its banks.

The walk back to the churchyard at Sydling St Nicholas passes a huge tithe barn Ⓓ, whose fine timbers now support a corrugated-iron roof. If you have time at the end of the walk, it is well worth exploring this gem of a village further. Waterside Lane, as its evocative name suggests, is particularly picturesque.

▶ *The view to the south from Reynards Copse, looking over rolling farmland dotted with sheep and cattle.*

The unusual raised wooden walkway gives you a great opportunity to see trees and birds from a different perspective. Tormentil (inset) flowers on the heath from May to September.

FACT FILE

- Moors Valley Country Park, 2½ miles (4km) west of Ringwood, off the A31

- Outdoor Leisure Map 22, grid reference SU 106057

  miles 0 1 2 3 4 5 6 7 8 9 10 miles
  kms 0 1 2 3 4 5 6 7 8 9 10 11 12 13 14 15 kms

- Allow 2½ hours

- Well maintained woodland tracks and a raised treetop path

- **P** Car park at the Visitor Centre

- **¶** Tea-room at the Visitor Centre

- **I** Visitor Centre, Tel. (01425) 470721 for details

A woodland walk from a country park through Ringwood Forest

Until 1984, Moors Valley Country Park was King's Farm on the banks of the Moors River. Now, the water feeds a new lake, and the main farm buildings have become the terminus for a narrow-gauge railway. Adjoining the country park, on the edge of Dorset heathland, is the much older Ringwood Forest. It was planted, mainly with pine trees, at the end of World War I.

Grey squirrels and sand lizards make their home in the forest, as do several species of birds, including the goldcrest, which feeds on insects in the young trees, and the crossbill, which searches among the older trees for cones, from which it extracts the seeds. Cuckoos can be heard in summer. Dawn and dusk are the best times to see the roe deer that live here, but they will melt away into the trees at the slightest unfamiliar movement or noise.

GIANT SCULPTURES

The walk begins at the country park's Visitor Centre **Ⓐ**, a 16th-century barn brought here from Gloucestershire and fitted with a floor from Wells Cathedral. Most visitors to the park do not go into the forest, but a short distance from the Centre is a Play Trail **Ⓑ** of giant sculptures made from logs cut in the forest. Andy Frost's models of snakes, spiders and crocodiles are part of a new Forestry Commission recreation scheme designed to encourage forest walks.

The Ashley Trailway Link, one of the main arteries through the forest, leads to the track-bed of the Southampton-Dorchester railway line, closed in 1974. The 145-year-old route has been reopened as a bridleway here and between Hamworthy and Wimborne, further down the

▼_In summer, the rides that run between the stands of conifers are good places to see butterflies flying and feeding._

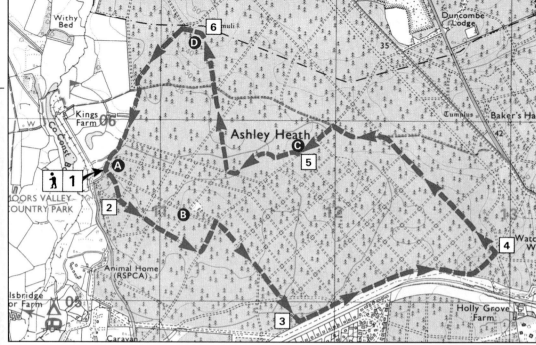

THE WALK

MOORS VALLEY — ASHLEY HEATH

The walk begins at the Moors Valley Country Park Visitor Centre Ⓐ.

1 Walk through a corner of the car park to the Forest Information Point, which is marked by yellow banners. Follow green waymarks along the metalled car park exit road to the Trailway Link.

2 Follow the straight and partly-gravelled path between mature trees with paths off to the left marked 'Play Trail' Ⓑ. At the end of the path, go left. At the next junction, turn right as indicated by the green waymark. When the main track swings away to the right, keep straight on, and continue ahead over the wide Horse Trail by the pond.

3 At a junction, a waymark in the middle of the now-narrow path points to the Ashley

line, as part of a long-term project to provide a long-distance route between Poole and the New Forest.

The walk runs parallel to the line for a while, before turning up Pine Avenue, the forest's longest straight track, which illustrates how varied a commercially managed woodland

Trailway. Turn left just before this waymark to leave the Trailway Link. Follow a path running parallel to the old railway line and along the edge of the forest. Later, the Horse Trail joins from the left. After a short, steep rise, bear half-left with the Horse Trail back into the forest. The wide grassy ride soon reaches a six-way junction.

4 Turn left onto a long, straight gravel track, Pine Avenue. Go straight on

can be. The route passes through cleared areas and new plantations as well as lines of mature trees.

The same point is made by the Tree Top Trail Ⓒ, a fenced wooden footpath rising to 14 feet (4.2m) above ground level. It goes between and above both well established and young trees. The narrow, twisting walkway has bays where you can stop and look and let others pass. By remaining still, and very quiet, you may well be able to observe bird and animal life from an unusual angle.

A steady climb leads to the Lookout Ⓓ, a shelter with a picnic table almost on the county border with Hampshire. From the wooden building there are extensive views to the south and west. A tall building in Bournemouth is visible on the southern horizon, while Hurn Airport, in the middle distance, is pinpointed by the planes landing and taking off. Ten miles (16km) to the south-west is the Tower Park

until the path climbs up to a foresters' hut. Go left at the hut onto a bridleway that briefly runs through a cleared area. At a crossroads, turn left and look for the entrance to the Tree Top Trail Ⓒ on your right.

5 Follow the gravel path of the Trail. After you come to a bend by a small clearing, the path is boarded, and rises rapidly up into the trees. At the far end of the path, go right and right again at a

water tower on Canford Heath; behind, 18 miles (30.8km) away, are the Purbeck Hills beyond Poole Harbour.

The wide path immediately below the Lookout runs down into the country park, crossing the old bridleway that was once the only public access to the woods. In the park, there is a wider range of trees, including oaks, birches and willows. Coots and kingfishers are found around Moors Lake. In winter, sheep are grazed in the park to maintain the heathland.

junction signposted to the Lookout Ⓓ.

6 Continue past the back of the Lookout on a path that winds downhill to a wide track. Turn left on this track alongside a cleared area. Go through two wooden gates. (If they are locked, either climb over them at the hinged end or take the path to the left and then turn right.) Beyond the gates, keep ahead between a young tree plantation and the golf course to the start.

STEAM RAILWAY

Beyond the golf course is a 7¼-inch(18.4-cm) narrow-gauge steam railway, the Moors Valley Railway. With 10 locomotives, it operates on weekends and school holidays, and on Sundays runs a walkers' shuttle between Kingsmere Station — the old King's Farm — and Lakeside, next to the Visitor Centre.

▲*At the Visitor Centre there is a picnic area and a wildlife pond with frogs, dragonflies and other water insects.*

BOB GIBBONS

DORSET

Explore the quarries and coastline of the Isle of Portland

The Isle of Portland is attached to the mainland by the shingle bank of Chesil Beach and a narrow causeway. The natural shelter of the beach was enhanced by great breakwaters, and a military dockyard was built on the northern shore. Before this, the island was best-known for its limestone (see box), used in some of Britain's finest buildings. Stone

MIKE WILLIAMS. INSET: STEPHEN DALTON/NHPA

FACT FILE

* ✳ Bill of Portland, 6 miles (9.6km) south of Weymouth, off the A354

* ⊙⩀ Pathfinder 1343 (SY 67/77), grid reference SY 677683

| miles 0 | 1 | 2 | 3 | 4 | 5 | 6 | 7 | 8 | 9 | 10 miles |
| kms 0 | 1 | 2 | 3 | 4 | 5 | 6 | 7 | 8 | 9 | 10 | 11 | 12 | 13 | 14 | 15 kms |

* ◑ Allow 3 to 4 hours

* ▬ Easy going on good paths and roads. Children must be carefully supervised near the cliffs

* P Car park at start

* T Regular bus service from Weymouth

* ⑪ A full range of facilities in Easton

* I For tourist information, Tel. (01305) 772444

▲ The Isle of Portland is littered with blocks of the famous Portland stone, which was lifted into barges with hand cranes (right). Portland is noted for rare birds and migrant butterflies, like the monarch (above left) from the USA.

appears everywhere; great slabs of it sit like building blocks in a giant's nursery, and small, irregular boulders are piled up to make dry-stone walls. In the sunshine, the stone shines a brilliant white.

This walk explores the southern half of the island, and begins near the Bill of Portland at the southern

MIKE WILLIAMS

THE WALK

BILL OF PORTLAND – EASTON

Begin at the car park at Bill of Portland.

1 Walk towards the lighthouse **A**, then turn left to follow the path along the coast (with the sea on your right) for about 1½ miles (2.4km), passing through an area of stone quarries **B**.

2 Where the track divides, continue following the line of the cliffs towards a house prominent on the horizon. When you reach a road, turn right.

3 Just beyond some strip fields **C**, turn right on a footpath that leads down towards Church Ope Cove. Follow the path behind some beach huts and climb the steps at the far side of the bay. Continue on under the arch of Rufus Castle **D**.

4 Turn right by the museum **E** onto a road, and follow it as it swings round to the left into the village of Easton.

5 Cross the square towards a church with twin spires. Turn left into Reforne. Go past Easton's post office, and continue on the road to the junction by St George's Church **F**. Turn right. Where the churchyard ends, take a path down through disused quarries **G** to the clifftop.

6 Turn left on the coastal

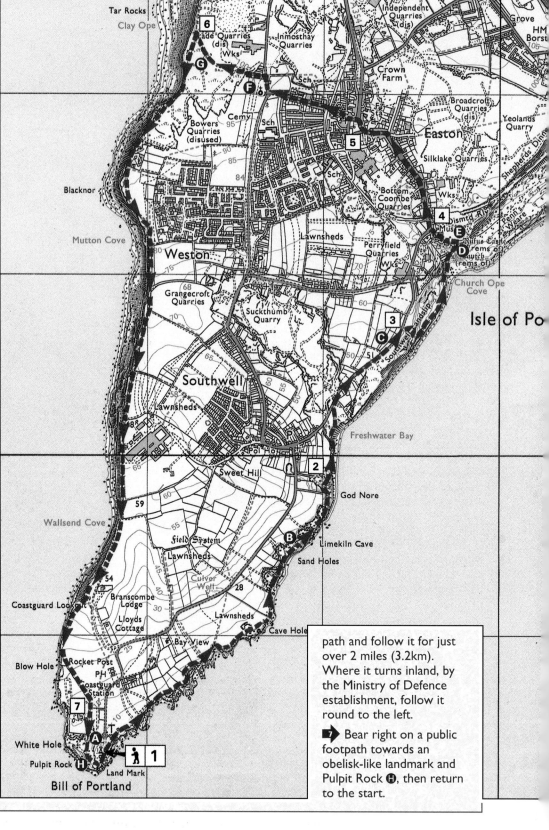

path and follow it for just over 2 miles (3.2km). Where it turns inland, by the Ministry of Defence establishment, follow it round to the left.

7 Bear right on a public footpath towards an obelisk-like landmark and Pulpit Rock **H**, then return to the start.

---

tip. The route heads straight for the lighthouse **A**, a dashing affair with bold red-and-white hoops. Built in 1906, the lighthouse replaced an earlier one that dated from 1789.

On it is a plaque from the original, declaring that it was built 'For the Direction and Comfort of Navigators'. The 18th-century lighthouse was the first to use lenses to concentrate the beams. One reason why the light was needed can be

seen out to sea; a tidal rip creates an area of rough water and white-capped waves, even on calm days.

The low cliffs extend out to sea as a series of flat ledges, the remains of quarries worked in the middle of the 19th century. The natural joints in the rock that made it possible to extract the stone in large blocks are clearly visible. On one ledge is a hand crane. Cranes like this once loaded stone into sailing barges, but

they are now used for raising and lowering small fishing boats. The area of the Bill had a large number of wooden huts and chalets, and a few huts are still used by the fishermen. Behind them is a row of former coastguard cottages.

The sea has eaten away at the rock ledges, leaving isolated stacks among the waves. A second lighthouse can be seen, and the top of a third beyond it. These two towers

ALL PHOTOS: MIKE WILLIAMS

part of Rufus Castle **D**. Begun by William II in the 11th century, it was largely rebuilt 100 years later.

At the end of the 18th century, the castle and surrounding land was given to John Penn, whose father, William, founded Pennsylvania. He built a splendid mock fortress, Pennsylvania Castle, at the top of the cliffs, and this is now a hotel.

FOSSIL WALL

The path from Church Ope emerges close by an excellent little museum **E** that tells the story of Portland. The route heads along the broad

were built in 1716, and originally had coal-fired lights. The nearer one is used as a bird observatory.

There is no shortage of bird life to watch as you walk along the clifftop; cormorants fish off the rocks and skylarks hover and sing above the grassland. On the high land at the centre of the island, a pattern of fields unchanged since the Middle Ages is visible. Huge fields were divided by banks and walls, known as lawnsheds, into strips, or lawns.

CLIFFTOP QUARRIES

At Cave Hole there is a large circular depression where a cave roof has collapsed. At the bottom are a number of stone blocks around which the crashing waves come swirling in. The view begins to open out across Weymouth Bay, which is lined by undulating chalk cliffs. The path enters an area of old quarry workings **B**, a fantastic landscape of piled stones and man-made ravines.

A small promontory runs out towards the cliff-edge, on top of which is a double line of pierced stone blocks. The holes, plugged with wood, held spikes that fixed a

▲The banks separating the cultivation strips in the medieval fields are still clearly visible in several places.

▶This portable steam engine, looking like something from the Science Museum, once provided power for the quarries.

railed track in place. Trucks of spoil were trundled along this crude railway and tipped over the cliff.

Where the cliffs fall sheer to the sea, the walk bears left to a road. Away to the left is a rusted portable steam engine, once used in the quarries but long since abandoned. Nearer the road is a working quarry, which produces stone aggregate. Beyond it is a superb example of the strip field system **C**. The fields of this one small island were once divided by some 2,700 strips.

A path leads down from the road to the stony beach of Church Ope, the favourite bathing place in Portland, then climbs steeply back up the cliffs to a little area packed with interest. From the top of the steps, you can look out to The Weares, a tumbled wilderness of rock above which the Portland Railway once ran.

You go through an arch that was

◀ St George's at Easton is, naturally, built of Portland stone, and surrounded by gravestones in the same material.

main street of Easton, bordered by houses of local stone, and crosses the line of the old Portland Railway, sunk in a deep cutting. A castellated house on the left boasts an extraordinary garden wall entirely made up of fossils, which range from curly ammonites to petrified wood.

GEORGIAN CHURCH

The village square is graced by an unusually ornate Methodist church, with a Wesleyan school of 1878 alongside it. From the square, the unusually named Reforne (probably a corruption of 'Reeve's horn') leads to the splendid Georgian Church of St George **F**, which was designed and built by a Portlander, Thomas Gilbert, whose grandfather was a quarry agent for Sir Christopher Wren. A new house was built at the same time for the parish clerk. This later became the George Inn, and is used for meetings of the Court Leet.

Leaving the town streets behind, the walk continues on a footpath through one of the most interesting of the old quarries **G**. At the bottom

are traces of what was once the most important transport system on Portland; rows of stone sleeper blocks show where a simple horse-drawn railway once ran.

The blocks lead out of the quarry onto a broad track along the cliffs. This was the Merchants' Railway, built in 1826. A multitude of little branches joined the main line from all the quarries along the route.

Today, the track bed makes an ideal footpath. The view is magnificent. Chesil Beach, once the only route between Portland and the mainland, stretches away into the far distance. To its east are the breakwaters that create the still waters of the naval base, above which

▲ *On the way back, the route passes through an archway of huge stone blocks, and there are good views (below left) of Chesil Beach and the mainland.*

helicopters hover and buzz.

The cliffs on the western side of the island are higher and more dramatic than those on the east. Those who want to pause to drink in the views can stop at a rather grand seat, made of huge chunks of stone.

STONE ARCH

All the way along this section of the walk are reminders of the old quarrymen. A track used for tipping spoil runs over an arch built up of huge, squared-off blocks. Beyond the arch, the path narrows and becomes stonier. Grooves in the rock mark the line of the old railway.

You emerge on grassland above the cliffs and head inland past the Ministry of Defence area. The old lighthouse, a stumpy little tower with what looks like a summerhouse on top, comes into view. This was once the home of Dr Marie Stopes, the birth control pioneer.

Finally, you head towards Pulpit Rock ❽, a sea-stack which until a century ago was a rocky archway. A slab leaning against it has footholds to provide a stony ladder for the adventurous to climb.

Portland Stone

The Isle of Portland is a great mass of limestone, which, at its best, is a beautiful, fine-grained white stone. Different strata of stone can be seen in the quarries that abound in the area. Below about a foot (30cm) of topsoil sit perhaps 10 feet (3m) of inferior stone before the big blocks appear. First is 'roach', a coarse-

Carthorses and steam traction engines were both used to move the stone blocks.

textured stone, then the valuable 'whitbed', fine-textured with a few shells. Below that is found 'basebed', reckoned to be the finest of them all.

Basebed is a very hard stone, and hence difficult to cut and remove. The stone did not really come into its own until the reign of Charles II. Sir Christopher Wren loved it, and used it for his city churches and, most famously of all, St Paul's Cathedral. It has been estimated that the great

architect took, in all, about a million tons of the stone to London.

When St Paul's was repaired in the 1970s, stone was again ordered from Portland. One of the original blocks ordered by Wren was found, and finally delivered to its intended destination, almost three centuries late. The quarries that are open today no longer provide good quality building stone; instead, most turn out humble crushed aggregate.

DORSET

CAROLINE BACON, INSET: STEPHEN DALTON/NHPA

FACT FILE

* Stourpaine, 2 miles (3.2km) north-west of Blandford Forum, on the A350

* **OS** Pathfinders 1300 (ST 80/90) and 1281 (ST 81/91), grid reference ST 860093

| miles | 0 | 1 | 2 | 3 | 4 | 5 | 6 | 7 | 8 | 9 | 10 miles |
| kms | 0 | 1 | 2 | 3 | 4 | 5 | 6 | 7 | 8 | 9 | 10 | 11 | 12 | 13 | 14 | 15 kms |

* Allow 3½ hours

* Mostly well defined paths on downland. One steep climb. Riverside path is muddy in wet weather

* **P** By the church at the start

* The White Horse in Stourpaine

* **I** For tourist information, Tel. (01258) 454770

Magnificent views from two hilltop forts and a riverside path

This varied walk visits several ancient sites in north Dorset. You begin by the church in Stourpaine. This was rebuilt in 1858, but contains a kneeling statue of an earlier vicar, who had it erected in 1670, a few years before he died.

In a field behind the church are some mounds **Ⓐ** — all that remain of a medieval building and a moat. The route follows a grassy track out of the village. It descends to ash woods that border the River Stour under the steep west slope of Hod Hill. Kingfishers nest along the river, and water-lilies grow in profusion.

You emerge onto a road, and soon turn left up a spur of Hambledon Hill. Where the track reaches level ground at the top of the hill, a wood is just visible on your left. This is one of the most extensive yew forests in Europe, and possibly had its origins in the Iron Age.

An area of rough ground at the edge of Coombe Wood indicates the boundaries of a neolithic settlement **Ⓑ**, predating the more obvious Iron

▲*Looking west from Hambledon Hill, you get an idea of the extent of the views the hill fort settlers had over the surrounding terrain. Devil's-bit scabious (inset) flowers in the fields.*

Age fortification on the northern heights of Hambledon Hill by 3,000 years. Where the trig point stands, there was once a large enclosure, and the neolithic dead were left to decompose in the open air in the surrounding ditches.

The hill fort **Ⓒ** was built in about 500BC. On the steep northern slopes, the indentations of hut circles can be made out in the turf. The fort was abandoned in AD43, when the 2nd Augusta legion, under Flavius Vespasian, who later became Emperor, invaded Dorset.

CLUBMEN HAMMERED

Its history did not end there. In August 1645, 2,000 locals, known as the Dorset Clubmen, assembled on Hambledon Hill under the leadership of the Rector of Compton Abbas. They opposed the forces of the Civil War, which were destroying their land. Their banners declared, 'If you offer to plunder or take our cattle, be assured we will bid you battle'. Cromwell thought

little of this protest, and put the Clubmen to flight with 50 well trained dragoons. A century later, James Wolfe trained his soldiers here in preparation for their capture of Quebec on the Plains of Abraham.

From the summit, there is a spectacular view across the Vale of Blackmore, once a huge tract of medieval forest. Today, the clay soils make this green fertile area the domain of the dairy farmer, just as it was in Thomas Hardy's day. Rising out of the vale to the north-east are Melbury Hill and Fontmell Down, which, with Hambledon Hill, mark the northern edge of the chalk band that runs across the county.

▼*As you follow the route out of the charming village of Stourpaine, you pass this Georgian farmhouse.*

CAROLINE BACON

THE WALK

STOURPAINE – HAMBLEDON HILL

The walk starts by Stourpaine's church. To reach it, turn off the A350 by the White Horse pub and turn left at the next crossroads.

1 In the field behind the church are the medieval earthworks **A**. Return to the crossroads, and turn left along a lane called 'Havelin'. At the end, turn right up Hod Drive. After ½ mile (800m), the path goes downhill and follows the river-bank for a further ½ mile (800m). Where the river bends to the left, the path continues through the woods to come to a road.

2 Turn right. After 200 yards (180m), turn left into a lane leading to Keeper's Cottage. Go immediately right through a metal gate into a field. Walk uphill, with the hedge on your left, to a barn at the top.

3 Turn left through a gate just beyond the barn. Keep the field boundary on your right-hand side and follow a track, which eventually veers right towards a wood.

4 Go through a metal gate and over rough ground, with the wood on your right, for 100 yards (90m). Immediately after a wicket gate, turn left. Walk uphill, with the fence on your left, to a trig point, the centre of a neolithic enclosure **B**. A path from here leads ahead to the Iron Age hill fort **C**. Return to the trig point. Turn left down a broad track. Continue through two metal gates to a stone wall enclosing a wood at the bottom of the hill.

5 To see Shroton **D**, turn left on the crossing track by the wall. Return to the walled wood and follow the track ahead by the wall, and then by iron railings. Continue round the corner of the wood to a metal gate marked 'private'. Turn right and walk beside the fence for 10 paces until a clear path emerges. Follow this path through two wicket gates in succession, then turn left down the edge of the field. After 400 yards (360m), climb a stile on your left and walk between two wire fences, down to the road.

6 Turn right along the A350. About 300 yards (270m) beyond a right turn signposted to Child Okeford, and immediately after a bend, turn right into a field through a metal gate. Follow the track uphill to a gate at the top, and a barn.

7 Turn right before the gate, by a National Trust sign, to Hod Hill Iron Age fort **E** and the Roman camp **F**. Return to the National Trust sign and turn right along the ramparts to the corner of the fort. Turn left, climb the stile and follow a tree-lined track downhill, then alongside a stream to a lane. Where this joins a road, turn right and continue ahead to Stourpaine's church.

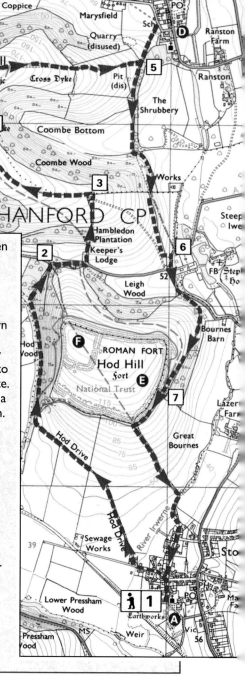

▲ *The northern slopes of Hambledon Hill have never been cultivated, so the ancient ramparts are clearly visible.*

CAROLINE BACON

Descending from the trig point, you reach a crossing track by a walled wood. To the left is the village of Iwerne Courtney or Shroton **D**. Shroton is the old part of the village, referred to in *Domesday Book* as 'Sheriff's town'. In 1261, it was granted a weekly market and a twice-yearly fair.

The church is true Gothic, rebuilt in 1610. It supposedly held 300 captured Clubmen overnight after their abortive stand on Hambledon Hill. Behind it are some unusual thatched barns. Shroton House, built in the 18th century, stands at the north end of the village.

To the south, as the route climbs Hod Hill **E**, another Iron Age fort, you pass through an entrance made by the Romans after they captured the fort in AD43. Roman ballistas were discovered in abundance near the remains of the largest Iron Age hut, suggesting they made a precise attack on the chief of the settlement.

The Romans built their own camp **F** in the north-west corner of the fort. It housed 600 infantrymen and 250 cavalrymen, and was in use until AD51. Many Iron Age and Roman objects have been found; most are now in the British Museum.

VARIOUS ORCHIDS

The southern slope of the hill fort has never been cultivated. This area of undisturbed chalkland is home to a range of orchids and a wide variety of butterflies, including the marsh fritillary. On the left side of the lane down into Stourpaine is a badger's sett, with runs radiating out into neighbouring fields. At the bottom is the River Iwerne, no more than a shallow stream, which you follow back into Stourpaine.

INDEX